LONELINESS: Living Between the Times

Nancy Potts

This book is designed for your personal reading pleasure and profit. It is also designed for group study. A leader's guide with helps and hints for teachers and visual aids (Victor Multi-use Transparency Masters) is available from your local Christian bookstore or from the publisher at $2.95. A Personal Involvement Workbook for private or group use is also available at $2.95.

VICTOR BOOKS

a division of SP Publications, Inc., Wheaton, Illinois
Offices also in Fullerton, California • Whitby, Ontario, Canada • London, England

ACKNOWLEDGEMENTS

Nothing is ever accomplished without the creative involvement and support of other people. I'd like to briefly acknowledge and express my gratitude to the following encouragers:

To Lloyd Potts for his patient perseverance and affirmation;

To Marilyn Hamor for typing the manuscript in spite of my spelling errors;

To John L. Petersen for giving me the opportunity to write on what sounded like an unbelievable subject;

To Norm Stolpe for providing answers to the "long-distance" questions, and editing the final manuscript;

To all those who have given me the gift of themselves with their struggles, fears, goals, and confrontations with loneliness.

Unless otherwise noted, all Scripture quotations are taken from the King James Version. Another version used is the *New English Bible* (NEB), © 1961, 1970 by The Delegates of the Oxford University Press and The Syndics of the Cambridge University Press.

Library of Congress Catalog Card Number: 78–51577
ISBN: 0-88207-630-2

VICTOR BOOKS
A division of SP Publications, Inc.
P.O. Box 1825 ● Wheaton, Illinois 60187

THE FAMILY CONCERN SERIES

This book is part of the Victor FAMILY CONCERN SERIES, a twelve-volume library dealing with the major questions confronting Christian families today. Each book is accompanied by a Leader's Guide for group study and a Personal Involvement Workbook for individual enrichment. All are written in a readable practical style by qualified, practicing professionals. Authors of the series are:

Anthony Florio, Ph.D., premarriage, marriage, and family counselor, *Two To Get Ready* (premarital preparation);

Rex Johnson, assistant professor of Christian education, Talbot Seminary, active in pastoral counseling (sex education and marriage preparation in the family);

Harold Myra, publisher of *Christianity Today* (sexuality and fulfillment in marriage);

J. Allan Petersen, speaker at Family Affair Seminars, *Conquering Family Stress* (facing family crises);

Nancy Potts, marriage and family counselor, *Loneliness: Living Between the Times* (dealing with personal loneliness);

Wayne Rickerson, family pastor, Beaverton Christian Church, Beaverton, Oregon and director of Creative Home Teaching Seminars, (family togetherness activities);

Wes Roberts, counselor in church and private practice and leader of marriage and family seminars (self-esteem);

Barbara Sroka, served on research and writing committees with Chicago's Circle Church and is active with their single adults, *One Is a Whole Number* (singles and the church);

Norman Stolpe, editorial director with Family Concern, Inc., (family goals);

James Thomason, assistant pastor at Calvary Baptist Church, Detroit, (family finances);

Ted Ward, Ph.D., professor and director of Values Development Education program at Michigan State University (value development in the family);

H. Norman Wright, assistant professor of psychology at Biola College and marriage, family, and child counselor, *The Family that Listens* (parent-child communication).

Consulting editor for the series is J. Allan Petersen, president of Family Concern Inc.

Contents

To
Sue and Boyd Needham
who gave me the gift
of life
and
Lloyd, Marilyn, Lanette
whose love and encouragement
made this work
possible

Foreword

Being alone is perhaps the most fundamental human predicament. It precedes even sin in the human experience. Everyone fears loneliness, and it does not go away when one is married or becomes a Christian. It can be acute even in the midst of a crowd. With courage, warmth, and insight, Nancy Potts helps us face ourselves with greater honesty. As a professional counselor working closely with a local church, she has lived with the loneliness of people of all ages. In helping others, she has reached into herself and out to God for the strength to accept this sometimes mysterious guest. Her wisdom and understanding is shared beautifully in this book.

This book is a significant part of Victor Books' Family Concern Series. In a time of great family consciousness and opportunity, many congregations are devoting increasing energies to family ministries. They have requested reliable and practical resources that speak to the needs of contemporary families. Victor Books and Family Concern have shared this vision and have cooperatively developed this comprehensive family ministry resource for churches.

The church relates to people throughout their lives, so it can help them whatever their point of need. The church, better than any other institution, can teach in greater depth the skills and concepts needed for healthy marriage and family relationships. The church can offer assistance and support at times of crises, because it has built in structures for education, enrichment, and problem solving.

This Family Concern Series has been carefully planned to capitalize on the unique abilities and opportunities churches have to minister to families. These 12 books are an encyclopedia of practical family information through which an individual can seek understanding. Pastors and other church professionals will find them invaluable for reference and counseling. Though each book stands alone as a valuable resource, study materials are also provided that they may be used in church and group settings. As a package, the Family Concern Series offers the congregation a thorough, long-term plan for adult family life education and the resources for meeting specialized family needs.

The resources in the Family Concern Series focus on the needs of three audiences: single adults, never married or formerly married, married couples—with or without children, and parents faced with child rearing responsibilities.

Each author in this series is a committed disciple of Jesus Christ, with a concern for the local church and with a high level of expertise in his/her subject. I am pleased with the enthusiastic cooperation of all these Christian leaders.

God uses people more than books to change people, so this Family Concern Series has been designed to help people work together on their family needs. A *Leader's Guide* has been prepared for each book in the series. It provides a group leader 13, one-hour plans for studying together. These may be used in adult Sunday school, Sunday evening, or mid-week study series, small informal study groups, and as seminars and workshops in conferences and retreats. These *Leader's Guides* include complete study plans, learning activity instructions, visual aids, and suggestions for further investigation and reading.

In addition to the *Leader's Guide,* a *Personal Involvement Workbook* accompanies each textbook, which enables each individual, whether studying in a group or alone, to get maximum benefit from the study. Each *Personal Involvement Workbook* includes the worksheets and activity instructions that are used in the group sessions as well as additional exercises for personal growth.

In studying each book as a group, the leader will need a *Leader's Guide* to gain maximum benefit, and each participant should have a *Personal Involvement Workbook.* Even in studying on your own or with your partner, you may want to get the *Leader's Guide* and start a group study yourself.

Since this Family Concern Series is a comprehensive resource, the needs felt by most families are included somewhere or several times in the series, even if the titles of the books may not so indicate. The chart on the following page has been prepared to help you find these specific issues in this book and in the other books in the series.

To write a "family encyclopedia" would make for dull reading, but this chart is a guide to the most important topics in each book and works as an index to the entire Family Concern Series. To find what you need, look down the alphabetical list of topics on the left side of the page. Then follow across the page to the right, noting the asterisks (*) under the titles across the top of the page, which will indicate that the book deals with the subject of interest to you.

This simple device ties the whole Series together. It is a road map that can help you get exactly what you need without being encumbered with a massive and complex index or cross-reference system. It also preserves the readability of the books. This chart plus the study materials make the Family Concern Series a powerful tool for you and your church in strengthening your family relationships.

A special word of thanks and appreciation goes to Norman Stolpe. As Family Concern's editorial director, his services were invaluable for this project. His vision and relationship with the various authors enabled the concept to take form in reality. His hard work brought the series from planning to completion.

I trust God will deeply enrich your life and family as you study and grow.

J. ALLAN PETERSEN
Family Concern
Wheaton, Ill.

GUIDE TO CURRICULUM SUBJECTS

‡ To be published in August 1979. All others currently available.

	Florio—Premarriage Two to Get Ready	Petersen—Crises	Potts—Loneliness Loneliness: Living Between the Times	Roberts—Self-esteem	Sroka—Singleness One Is a Whole Number	Wright—Communication	Johnson—Sex Education ‡	Myra—Sex in Marriage ‡	Rickerson—Fun & Togetherness ‡	Stolpe—Goals ‡	Thomason—Finances ‡	Ward—Values Development ‡
adolescent children		*		*		*	*		*	*		*
birth control	*						*	*		*		
child development				*		*	*		*			*
child discipline				*		*				*		*
child communication		*		*		*	*		*	*		*
church-family			*		*					*		*
dating	*				*		*					
death		*	*									
divorce		*	*		*							
emotions	*	*	*	*	*	*		*				
engagement	*	*						*				
finances		*									*	
friendship			*		*							
goals	*		*		*					*	*	
leisure			*		*				*	*		
loneliness			*		*				*			
marital communication	*	*	*						*		*	
marital conflicts	*	*							*		*	
modeling		*		*		*	*		*	*		*
role adjustment	*	*			*		*	*		*		
self-identity	*	*	*		*		*	*				
sex education	*	*					*	*				
sex in marriage	*							*				
value development							*			*		*
worship									*	*		*

1

Loneliness in All Seasons

I have traced and retraced the guideposts of my life, searching for the crisis that initiated my personal journey with lonely times. Certainly, I was introduced to loneliness during family crises, a major illness, and unexpected deaths. But I discovered that loneliness isn't only associated with crisis; I can turn any corner in the routine of my life and face it anew.

I'm especially in touch with my personal loneliness during events that touch me deeply: the beauty yet the finality of a sunset, moving to another city, the realization that friendships aren't always permanent, or seeing an elderly woman hobbling on tired legs. I remember the elderly woman well. She was seeking employment to supplement her retirement income. I heard her explain to a gift shop owner that she'd been a widow for about two months. She needed extra money to make ends meet. I watched in silent anguish as the owner turned her away. Sometimes a lonely fog engulfs me when I empathize with the disappointment another human being feels.

Scripture reveals the pangs of loneliness in the passages of life. The people whose lives are recorded throughout these pages had experiences which intersect with everyone's daily joys and sorrows. Even Christ spoke of lonely isolation when He cried from the cross, "My God, My God, why hast Thou forsaken Me?" (Matt. 27:46) Rejection, or the fear of it, can immediately trigger feelings of lonely emptiness.

As a marriage and family counselor, I've witnessed loneliness within marriage, isolation during divorce, sorrow after the death of a family member, and fears of some of the never-married who desperately want an intimate relationship. Other passages also underscore our solitary nature. Life's promotions can be haunting times of self-evaluation. The transitions from adolescence into the 20s, the 20s into the 30s, the 30s into the 40s, and so on, are laced with bittersweetness. A time to say good-bye to one cycle of life and begin another one. Loneliness is a companion that comes at birth and leaves at death. It is a fact of life.

The loneliness borne of crisis can awaken terror, but the loneliness of everyday living is just as powerful. Cultivating those feelings and discovering their value occurs one moment at a time. Tho choice of what to get out of the experience measures its worth.

Current literature doesn't explore loneliness in the lives of Christians. I wonder why, since loneliness is a natural process of life. The church community responds to some crises that provoke loneliness, such as a member's bereavement. But the everyday experiences of loneliness are overlooked. The Bible is filled with circumstances which arouse lonely feelings: The shepherd, alone with his flock; the disciples, who left families behind to follow Jesus; the prodigal son, as he asked his father for hired-hand status; and Christ, who felt the anguish of impending death.

Biblical history is replete with instances that trigger loneliness: the death of a loved one, rejection, abandonment, isolation, disappointment, failure, alienation from God, even the awareness that each of us is alone. So why isn't it in current Christian literature?

Perhaps too many Christians have taken a stand that faith should be a cure for loneliness and church fellowship a preventative for being alone. Or maybe parallels have not been drawn between the language and times of the Bible and today's world. Shepherds are no longer common, that's true. But business executives tend corporations in concrete cities. Families divide for innumerable reasons . . . death, divorce, moving to another city or country. Mobility creates feelings of isolation and loneliness.

Faith *will* not insulate us from loneliness. Quite the contrary. Christians who expose themselves invariably take a stand in life. Convictions have a price tag. And to respond to people with love in His name risks vulnerability. Rather than preventing loneliness, faith gives a foundation for understanding it. Fellowship offers the opportunity not to be alone, though being alone and loneliness are not the same.

Because loneliness has been viewed as synonymous with failure, the terror is felt more than the beauty of those painful moments. As one woman said, "I'd tell a friend if I was happy or sad or hurt. But to say, 'I'm lonely'? My friend would wonder why no one wanted to be around me."

Christians are human, open to love and loss and the experiences of life. Loneliness is a natural process of life; an uncomfortable, painful, restless experience, perhaps. But in a lonely experience you can learn lessons about yourself, your relationships, and your faith in God. The journey can begin wherever you are in life, with whatever personal baggage that's labeled with your name. The experience can be one of personal growth and celebration or one of paralyzing terror. How do you choose to live *your* loneliness?

Roots

Loneliness has its roots in a kaleidoscope of experiences. Unfulfilled promises, broken relationships, career disappointments, heated arguments with God, feelings of rejection, and the uncertainty of tomorrow. Life is more than birth to death with only space in between. The cycles of life will not permit a static position for long. As I searched my personal solitude, I met others who shared with me the reality of their loneliness.

A woman in Houston described her struggle for self-acceptance. She summed up her adult years in one word: *frustration*. She saw her life as average and predictable. Her daydreams centered around her desire to be someone else. When she returned for her 20-year high school reunion, she faced the question, "And what are you doing now?" Her answer was an empty, "Nothing." She wasn't writing the great American novel; she wasn't in demand as a speaker; housework didn't fulfill her; she sang off-key; and she often felt lonely in a crowd. Even her children didn't turn out to be all that she'd hoped. She always had good ideas . . . too late. Alex Haley wrote *Roots* before she developed an interest in genealogy; she volunteered her house for the Sunday School party five minutes after someone else had offered hers. So went the story of her life.

Loneliness followed her around like a cloud as she searched for ways to feel good about herself. Eventually this woman began to like herself, but only when she could acknowledge her lonely times and use them as an opportunity to learn more about herself. The question she struggled with was, "Can I accept myself for what I am?"

Her life contrasted with that of a successful business executive. John described his life as one full of change. "I'm never the same from one day to the next," he explained. "As I look at my relationships, I discover that I have admirers, companions, business associates, a nice family, and church cronies but no friends. I've been too busy to confide in anyone, and I've paid the price. Even my old friends have gradually become strangers." John told his story by retracing the steps of his life. He recounted the deep pockets of loneliness that preceded times of decision-making. Even when he described his career and his family relationships as fulfilling, he repeated the theme. "But sometimes I feel so *lonely*. And regardless of good relationships, fond memories, and success, I can't escape from those feelings. They punctuate my daily existence.

"My colleagues consider me successful, my Sunday School class views me as devout, and my family knows I'm devoted to them. How surprised they'd be to hear that still I struggle to overcome the part of myself that I keep a secret . . . I'm lonely."

John's story is not unusual. A woman in her early 30s, recently divorced, shared her biggest hurdle. "I can't identify with success and fulfillment. But I can feel the pain of loneliness. I still want to discover a lot about myself. In the mornings, I silently replay memories while drinking coffee and living through anxiety attacks. I have questions that haunt me—How can I get through this? What good can come from it? Is such profound loneliness normal?

The questions are as natural as the feelings that each of us may confront at different times and in varying ways. There's no pill to swallow for loneliness. In fact, if there were, the impetus to investigate our own solitude would be lost.

Loneliness Is a Challenge

Most people are more acquainted with the power of loneliness than with what loneliness is. Certainly, it's a statement of who we are—creatures created by God, responsible for ourselves and to Him. Loneliness is synonymous with being human. A crisis is usually the pivotal point, when we recognize that each of us is a solitary, unique individual. Then we realize that no one else can provide us with the answers to the deepest questions of life. To be suddenly awakened to the terror and isolation in loneliness can trigger the desire to run from the experience and from oneself. To be open to lonely moments is a profound challenge that makes possible deeper relationships to others and to God.

Life offers many paradoxes. Loneliness can be a time for growth only after you are willing to live with the painful feelings and explore their meaning. You must travel with the discomforts in order to receive the gift of greater self-awareness, deeper friendships, and a more mature faith.

Loneliness is not an idea, but a voyage; not an enemy, but a natural condition of life; not a withdrawal from God, but a step closer to Him; not a retreat, but a process toward a greater awakening to life. It can be a time for reviewing old patterns, searching silent questions, and facing the realities of life—if you choose to use it in these ways.

Obviously, the experience is demanding. It taxes inner resources, and beckons you to view loneliness as something to embrace rather than escape. There is no way to stamp out loneliness or discover a solution for it. In fact, such an expectation will lead to despair. Our task is to learn to accept it, live with it, and use it creatively. No one can live long without becoming acquainted with loneliness. And with loneliness comes opportunity for hope, joy, and being related.

Throughout the Old and New Testaments, God offers assurances that life has a meaning. The message in the Scriptures offers directions and lessons applicable today. People are usually more aware of the suffering quality in loneliness than of the value in it, but you have only to turn to Ecclesiastes for a different understanding. There you will discover a vivid picture of the naturalness of grief and the relationships between loneliness and wisdom.

I said to myself, "I have amassed great wisdom, more than all my predecessors on the throne in Jerusalem; I have become familiar with wisdom and knowledge." So I applied my mind to understand wisdom and knowledge, madness and folly, and I came to see that this too is chasing the wind. For in much wisdom is much vexation, and the more a man knows, the more he has to suffer.

(Ecc. 1:16-18, NEB)

For everything its season, and for every activity under
heaven its time:
a time to be born and a time to die;
a time to plant and a time to uproot;
a time to kill and a time to heal;
a time to pull down and a time to build up;
a time to weep and a time to laugh;
a time for mourning and a time for dancing;
a time to scatter stones and a time to gather them;
a time to embrace and a time to refrain from embracing;
a time to seek and a time to lose;
a time to keep and a time to throw away;
a time to tear and a time to mend;
a time for silence and a time for speech;
a time for love and a time to hate;
a time for war and a time for peace.

(Ecc. 3:1-8, NEB)

All seasons of our lives offer value and potential discovery.
Begin to tune in to yourself. As you live out today and begin
tomorrow, be sensitive to those times that feel uncomfortable.
Before you try to escape, experience the feelings and their
messages to you. Do you feel isolation, abandonment, rejection, or loss? Try to give a name to the discomfort or the pain.
Write down what and how you feel. Acknowledgment is the
first step in coming to terms with the lonely part of yourself.
The lessons to be learned will not occur overnight, and you
won't suddenly see the value in loneliness. It's a process that
spans the seasons of life.

Living Your Loneliness

During the day or week, respond to these questions from your
own experience:
1. What is loneliness?
2. When was the last time you felt lonely?
3. How do you feel when you're lonely?

2

Rites of Passage

The question, "What is loneliness?" has to be answered from one's own experiences. It is a thread woven into the fabric of all our lives. It is more obvious with some people than with others. But the thread is there, regardless of how noticeable it is. Responses to the question have been revealing. Being able to express the feelings provides an opportunity to break through the walls we've erected to hide our fears. Here are several responses from people learning to live with their lonely times:

1. "To me, being alone means being *afraid*. I'm scared of what the feelings will do to me. When I feel myself sinking, I try to stay busy. It's feeling empty, washed-out, tired of everything. It's wanting to be with someone, anyone, but not really caring to search for someone. It's a thinking period."

2. "When I think of loneliness, I feel abandoned. It reminds me of being hospitalized when I was fourteen. When visiting hours were over, the nurses ushered out my parents, my sister and brother, and my friends. Sometimes I'd wake up in the middle of the night and cry myself back to sleep. I knew they hadn't deserted me. But, at three in the morning,

in the still darkness, my emotions played tricks on me."

3. "Being lonely means *failure* and *rejection*. I grew up thinking that loneliness was a bad emotion. It was something nice people, especially Christians, didn't have. When I was fired from my job several years ago, I felt desperately, painfully lonely. I thought my world had ended. I felt rejected and not wanted by anyone. And I felt guilty for feeling so low. I didn't think any of my friends wanted to be around me, so I withdrew. Actually, *I* couldn't face *them!* I discovered that running from myself didn't erase the fact that I felt rotten and worthless."

4. "Loneliness, to me, is grief. When a good friend dies or moves away, I feel an overwhelming loss. I never know what the feelings are, much less what to do with them. Usually, I cry and am depressed. I plead with God and pray that He will remove the pain, but it doesn't always happen the way I plan."

5. "I feel lonely even when traumatic events aren't occurring. Just my everyday, routine schedule has lonely moments tucked in it."

6. "Loneliness is being in a leadership position. It's being the one to make clutch decisions, realizing I'll be criticized regardless of what decision I make. It's not knowing whether people like me for who I am or for what I can do for them because of my position. Being lonely is an endurance contest."

The stories are common—people trying to understand their feelings and obtain a clearer perception of themselves.

Transition Periods

Numerous unobserved rites mark the passage between birth and death. Our society singles out a few transitions for recognition—birth, the beginning of the teenage years, marriage, the birth of a child, age 40, retirement, and death. Traditionally, age 21 marked the official passage into adulthood. But now that states consider 18 as the legal age, there's confusion over the appropriate time for the "celebration of adulthood." In coming years, that rite of passage may be eliminated altogether.

Throughout life, everyone experiences "little griefs" scattered among the major transitions, but most of us are not as familiar with the tremendous impact the "small deaths" have. We're more accustomed to following the accepted rituals for birth, marriage, or death. When a family member dies, survivors are encouraged to grieve. Feelings of loss and loneliness are accepted and understood. For the Christian, death is saying good-bye only to someone's physical life. But it signals the beginning of a new cycle of life for the family members and close friends left behind. They must reorganize their lives without the presence of the one who died.

When Jesus died on the cross, His disciples and friends grieved, tried to determine their next step, and talked about the One who'd been crucified. Jesus' resurrection was a time of tremendous joy, but again the disciples had to say good-bye. This time it was to His physical presence on earth. This ushered in the next cycle of life for the followers of Christ. Transitions; good-byes; grief; new beginnings; we understand how to respond to rites of passage.

The Small Deaths

Because we're not accustomed to accepting the little griefs as natural periods of loss, we're not prepared to openly face them, and learn from them. As one woman explained, "When my dearest friend moved to another city, I felt helplessly lonely. It was as though part of me died. I tried to explain how I felt to another friend, but she didn't understand. She said she did, but when she told me I'd get over it in time, I realized she didn't appreciate my loss. People always try to fix everything or explain it away. What I really needed was for someone to understand my pain. I then could cry my tears and feel acceptable."

Many situations trigger feelings of loss and loneliness. Learning to deal with the little griefs better enables us to face and move through major losses when they occur. Acknowledging the uncelebrated rites of passage can help us to face ourselves and to be alert to some of the triggers for loneliness. Here is a selection of predictable experiences which are passages of living. Naturally, your response to any one of these may be different than someone else's, depending on the circumstances in your life.

Parents give birth to a child. The occasion is one of celebration. But when parents realize how much a baby alters their life-style, they may feel a gnawing loneliness tugging at them. Energy, time, attention, and freedom are changed in the midst of celebrating a new addition to the family.

The birth of another child. This occasion makes additional demands on the parents, and on the children already in the family, who often wonder if they're loved as much, since so much attention is given to the new baby.

Childhood disability or illness. This triggers parents' feelings of helplessness to prevent the pain of their child. Hospitalization can be agony for the child as well as for parents separated from him by doctors, nurses, rules, and clinical apparatus. Lack of control over events breeds loneliness.

The first child enters school. Parents may have feelings of separation even while they are excited about new learning experiences. They may sense a loss of total influence on their child's life. The peer group and teachers begin a never-ending influence, and there's no going back to infancy.

Further education. Each movement from day-care center to kindergarten to elementary school to middle school to high school to college is a link in a chain of more independence. Parents may feel gratitude that their children are becoming adults but, at the same time, an awareness dawns that child-rearing days will end.

Marriage. The marriage relationship's first face with reality triggers loneliness if expectations for marriage and the image you had of your spouse are not all that you thought. Facing loneliness and disappointment can be the first steps toward negotiating a realistic, healthy relationship.

Loss of friendships. Friendships change through geographic distance, loss of common ties, or misunderstanding.

Job loss. Being out of work can be lonely, regardless of the reason.

Moving. A move to another city is considered to be one of the most traumatic changes in people's lives. Children must reestablish themselves. A husband may be immersed in a new job while his wife is alone, sorting out her new identity in unfamiliar surroundings.

Birthdays. The age marked by an adult's birthday isn't as significant as the meaning it has for him.

Major illness. Illness brings an awareness of the lack of control one has over life and death.

Unfulfilled dreams. These prompt a first awareness of what might have been if other choices had been made.

First dates of children. To parents, these are announcements that their children will make their own lives. Parents wonder if they'll be ready, if they have done all they can do in preparation, and if the children will repeat or avoid the mistakes they made.

Death of a pet. The death of a pet often highlights loneliness, even for adults.

Great expectations. Loneliness comes when you feel misunderstood or expectations in a relationship aren't met.

Gossip. The first time you're aware that you're the recipient of the latest gossip is a startlingly lonely moment.

Career changes. Changes of careers plunge many into loneliness.

Self-perception. Loneliness comes when you first realize that how you view yourself is different from how others see you.

Early achievers. Those who reach career/financial/social goals early in life question, "Where to from here?"

Leadership. Loneliness is inherent in leadership and decision-making positions.

Empty-nest syndrome. This starts when the children are grown. You and your spouse are a family alone for the first time in over 20 years. Some prepare for the change and greet the transition with anticipation. Others are shocked by the impact, and fear they no longer have anything in common with their mate. Children marry, and/or become involved with their careers. Reestablishing relationships on an adult level is difficult if you're a parent who has lived your life through your children. You're on your *own* now!

Divorce. Divorce involves enormous grief, loss, and loneliness.

Grandparents. If you become a grandparent, you notice your children spend more time with *their* children than with you. Christmas celebrations may now move to their houses. Perhaps a joyful occasion, but underlying is an awareness that life goes on.

Death of friends. Good friends die sooner than you expected.

Physical changes. Such changes prompt the recognition of additional limitations. The desire to prove youthfulness to yourself or other people, to recapture dreams, or to reevaluate how you spent your time may accompany the aging process.

A realization of age. This happens the first time you hear someone refer to "the old people" and realize that you're one of them.

A dream house. Loneliness can occur when you move to a dream house or apartment and realize that it doesn't solve all your problems.

Singleness. Loneliness may be a problem if you do not marry, and have to deal with disappointment and the expectations of other people, as well as your own.

Childlessness. Remaining childless for any reason other than by choice can be devastating.

After a year. The year anniversary of the death of a loved one is solitary.

Anniversaries. If you feel you have nothing to celebrate, anniversaries can be lonely.

Terminal Illness. Loneliness can come from being with someone who is terminally ill. You can care, but that doesn't remove the pain.

Evaluation of faith. The first major evaluation of your faith, and each subsequent one, underscores that you are human. Not every question will have answers nor can you control all the events of your life.

Retirement. This could involve financial, home, or location changes, depending on circumstances.

Certainly, additional experiences activate loneliness. Looking at old scrapbooks; entering a dark, empty house; getting lost on the freeway—all are examples of situations which drive you into the lonely part of yourself.

The list at first glance may cause you to think of life as a continual time of loss and loneliness. Granted, life *is* problem-solving. Recognizing the stages of life and learning to deal with the potential loneliness, frees you to experience the joy, hope, and fulfillment in life. That's the paradox of looking into your identity as a solitary individual. By looking inward, you have a greater capacity to relate upward and outward.

No One Is Immune

Many people assume that loneliness happens only to other people and that success, marriage, financial security, or "something" else is an antidote to being lonely. Biblical truth, however, reveals that no one is immune to loneliness. Not in Bible times, nor in the 20th century.

Numerous examples could be explored, but one of the most powerful expressions is evidenced in the lives of two very different people—Jesus and Judas. We often presume that since those in public life are surrounded by people, they're spared from lonely anguish. However, anyone who holds a position of responsibility or expresses strong convictions must contemplate the lonely nature of existence.

Matthew wrote that Judas returned the 30 silver pieces to the high priest after Jesus' death. According to his words, he'd condemned an innocent man. Judas, the traitor, threw the money down in the temple and later hanged himself (Matt. 27:3-5). His misery and remorse drove him to self-destruction. Judas was exposed to condemnation and rejection on all sides. The chief priests didn't trust him; they used him. His fellow disciples condemned him. He knew misunderstanding and grief, but Judas also made his choices and lived with their consequences. The One who could have forgiven him was the One he helped execute. Although he could have sought forgiveness, he chose suicide instead. Few can bear the constant torment of condemnation, regardless of the rightness or wrongness of the crusade. With no one was Judas acceptable or welcome, least of all to himself.

Jesus was no stranger to loneliness either. His cause and purpose did not spare Him from the weight of suffering. He went to the Mount of Olives with His disciples to pray, for the time of His crucifixion was near (Luke 22:39-51). He prayed that if there was any way to accomplish God's purpose without facing the coming events, God would "take this cup away." The gentle Messiah returned from prayer to find His disciples asleep, and to the loneliness of being misunderstood, mistrusted, receiving physical and verbal insults, and of being betrayed by a kiss. Jesus could understand loneliness because He'd lived with it throughout His life. Search the Scriptures to discover that He had His own struggles. From birth to physical death, He realized that no one but the Father could completely understand Him.

Jesus and Judas were two men with different purposes: One

came to save the world, the other to become a traitor. Both were crusaders but for different goals; both felt deserted. Neither was understood by the people closest to him; each grieved; each had choices about how to handle the terror in loneliness. One discovered you can't destroy another without doing the same to yourself. The other chose to follow the way of the cross and life eternal.

The Prophet Isaiah and John the Baptist echo the words, "Prepare ye the way" (Isa. 40:3; Matt. 3:3). Learning to live with the little griefs helps to prepare us to deal with the ultimate, more painful ones. Jesus was prepared. He prayed and grieved when friends died; He felt pain for unbelievers. He knew the meaning of rejection. His whole life was preparation, so that at the final moment He was able to face the next rite of passage.

Dag Hammarskjold in *Markings* said, "Pray that your loneliness may spur you into finding something to live for, great enough to die for." Each of us, in varying degrees and intensities, lives with the loneliness of being a solitary individual called on to face life's experiences. How are you living with the little griefs in your life?

Living Your Loneliness

During the day or week, respond to these questions from your own experience:

1. Follow your day-to-day patterns this week. How do you relate to any loss, large or small, that you experience?

2. List your own rites of passage that were not on the sample list. How have you handled loss up until now? Have your methods changed with the experiences?

3

Experience versus Existence

The letter was from a woman in her early 30s. She lived in a suburban community surrounded by neighbors and the latest conveniences, and she followed the prescribed rules of conduct. People around her appeared to be happy, or at least that was the mask they wore. Since she was unable to be spontaneous and real in the presence of others, she seldom enjoyed intimate companionship. Relationships often were an act of impersonal convenience rather than meaningful relatedness.

Her letter was a story about herself and the isolation of her existence:

I'm so tired of the loneliness of life. I wonder if anyone else knows what it means to be in such pain. I surround myself with people only to experience the old cliché of being "lonely in a crowd." I try to sleep, but my head splits with a headache. I know my husband and children are asleep; I can hear the sounds, and the rhythm of their breathing. My family doesn't understand me. They think they do, but it's based on opinions and statements I made a long time ago.

My biggest need is to be accepted as I am, for who I

27

am. But I don't even know what I'm like. I feel like an accumulation of the roles I fill. I wonder if I even have an identity apart from wife, mother, chauffeur, and cook. It's so difficult to accept my life as it is. There will always be constant struggles to face problems, learn about myself, and stand up for my convictions.

I'm so tired of the agonizing loneliness. I'm afraid of it, but I can't seem to eat, sleep, or schedule the feelings away. I have to choose life. I can no longer postpone dealing with the anxiety of straddling the fence. None of my education prepared me for the amount of solitude there is in life. No amount of security can eradicate painful experiences. Why was I never taught to learn from loneliness? I only learned to fear it.

The letter was written to herself. Rather than huddling on the couch, a victim of insomnia, she wrote a diary of her feelings. She discovered, with the loss of her own pretenses, that she's not immune to the loneliness that's part of existence. Society may reward successful people, but even success is not a panacea for loneliness.

Two Types of Loneliness

There are two types of the human condition called loneliness: one is the loneliness borne of existence; the other is borne of the experiences of life. The loneliness of existence begins at birth. Not as the result of something a person does, but as a condition of being alive. The original awareness of separation from God, from others, and from oneself has its origin in the Christian understanding of sin.

The diary of a lonely woman depicts the existence quality. Courage was required for her to face her essential loneliness. She alluded to ways she'd tried to escape her feelings but learned that doing so only alienated her from other people and herself. In fact, it seemed to desensitize her from her own feelings. Because she decided to face her fear, she took the initial step to further her own growth, sensitivity, and creativity.

Loneliness can be a parenthesis around the developmental phases of our lives. The deepest, most profound experiences of life are yours alone to live with, make sense of, and deal with.

"I seldom feel acute loneliness," a friend shared, but she described a hospital scene in which this had been the case.

"I had a friend who died of cancer at the age of 30. They discovered it two years ago, and she had a mastectomy. I can still remember the conversation we had after her diagnosis.

" 'I'm scared,' Carrie had said. 'My first reaction to the diagnosis was not to believe it. How could it be *me?* I'm six months pregnant and have my whole life ahead of me. Why? How could I have cancer *now?*'

"Her eyes searched mine for an answer, or at least a response, and I said, 'I'm sorry.' I wish I'd left it there, but I quickly added, 'I understand.'

" '*Understand?* How can *you* understand?' blazed Carrie. 'You're well and strong, and can wake up in the morning without wondering how much of your body has deteriorated during the night. You won't lose a part of yourself through surgery. How can you understand?'

"I realized the truth in her words. I cared; I ached inside. But I couldn't understand, not really. I hadn't been there. When my visit with Carrie was over, I drove to the beach. As I walked in the sand, the tears streamed down my face. Waves crashed against the shore, and I felt stark loneliness. I hadn't been able to comfort my friend. I couldn't even understand my own reactions.

"Toward the end of the day, the sky turned deep shades of pink, purple, and gold. The sun was saying good-bye. Once again the pangs of loneliness wrenched my heartstrings. Some things only my deepest self can experience: the fear of cancer, the death of a loved one, the birth of a child, even the beauty and mystery of a sunset.

"I don't feel extreme loneliness often. But I do understand it. For I've been there."

Understanding Another's Loss

Watching another person face loneliness is disturbing. If you have a friend who plunges into solitary pain, you often try to provide remedies to help him escape. Perhaps you attempt to plan a hectic social life, surround him with a crowd, or talk him out of his depression. In any event, since you're not comfortable with your own loneliness, you find it difficult to permit someone else his or hers. In essence, you contribute to your friend's loneliness and self-alienation by giving him the message that his feelings are unacceptable. Since you regard personal pain as destructive, you too often rush in to rescue the "victim."

If you don't appreciate the value in loneliness, you won't understand that the solution for it is to accept and face it. Only by living with it can you learn to develop the inner resources to turn it into a creative experience.

A minister was involved in a hunting accident which cost him the use of his right eye. During his recovery from having a plastic eye inserted, he underwent intense feelings of loss and the loneliness of not being understood. Other ministers, friends, and people in his congregation couldn't bear to see his sullenness. So they told him it was God's will, everything would be OK, or it could have been worse. No one seemed comfortable hearing him express his real feelings. So he bottled them up, and felt increasingly unacceptable. One day he received a letter from a minister in another state. The message was short and simple: "I heard you lost your eye. It's really a shame. I'm sorry." That was all, but it broke the dam of pent-up emotions. Tears flowed. Finally, he could cry because someone understood his loss.

In attempting to overcome a fear of loneliness, you can overreact into escapism. Running from yourself with overly busy schedules, self-criticism, or a desperate search for relationships can breed feelings of inferiority. Eventually, you may develop a personal identity that isn't defined realistically. In such cases, poor self-esteem can motivate you to place other people's wants and expectations over your own. Your identity then becomes so confused that not only are your needs second to other people's, but you may lose grasp of what you realistically do need. It becomes a vicious, self-destructive cycle. Running from uncomfortable feelings breeds a loss of identity that will separate you further from yourself, other people, and God.

The Prodigal Son
Nowhere is this more apparent than in the story of the Prodigal Son (Luke 15:11-24). The results of loneliness are exposed in the lives of all concerned.

As the story begins, the younger son clearly displays his dissatisfaction with the limits of his life. He wanted to join the rest of the world and leave the authority of his father; consequently, he demanded that his father give him his share of the inheritance. Presumably, he wanted all that would be his after his father's death. Surprisingly, the father granted his wish, and his younger son left to live a different life-style. However, he wasn't prepared to fully confront life as it really was.

The son who believed he could surmount any obstacle discovered he was only human after all. Realities aren't negotiable. In a relatively short amount of time, he had no money and was forced to feed someone else's pigs in order to survive. Even his father's workers had it better! From seeking total freedom and independence, the prodigal returned home, seeking the status of a hired helper and total dependency. Now he wanted to serve the authority figure he previously resented.

Not satisfied with who he was before, he now wanted to fill a role just as unrealistic. From the idea that he could do all things, he'd retreated to the notion that he deserved to do nothing. He was polarized in opposite directions with neither extreme representative of his identity.

Then comes the next surprise. The loving father, who was wise enough to allow his son to learn lessons for himself, even the painful ones, now refused to be manipulated. His son had learned a lesson on limits. He wasn't going to undo it by treating his son as a weak child, incapable of making decisions. The prodigal son was challenged by an accepting father to mature in his identity. Just think about the profound implications. To be punished for a mistake is sometimes easier than to be greeted with understanding. The father's love was unconditional. Consequently, the son who was alienated from himself, his family, and his God had to look into himself and discover who he was, what inner resources he possessed, and how to deal with the loneliness in his life.

In each situation of loneliness, you can't respond to another person until you first learn from its lessons yourself. You can't appreciate your own uniqueness if you run from your feelings. You can't be intimately related to people or to God until you make time to learn about your own limits and potential. Alienation is the price of escapism. Each of us packs his own bags for the journey through life and we're responsible for our choices along the way. What baggage are you carrying with you?

Living Your Loneliness
During the day or week, respond to these questions from your own experience:

1. When you think of your own lonely times, what scares you about the experience?
2. What are your limitations and your potential?

4

Alone versus Lonely

The flip side of wanting to be related to people contains its
own truth. Everyone has times when they need to be alone.
Most are better able to recognize this need in themselves than
in other people. If a friend or family member chooses to be
alone at a time when your preference is otherwise, you may
create a climate of guilt. Refusing to allow a person to meet
his own privacy needs is a statement that the relationship
exists only to meet your needs. The other person invariably
feels manipulated and unappreciated as an individual.

If you feel that being alone is unpleasant, you may grant
the privilege to those closest to you only with difficulty. Yet
all people need a balance in their lives—a time to be alone
and a time with people. Most people live on either extreme
rather than with a balance. Either they constantly strive to be
surrounded by people, and thereby sacrifice their aloneness,
or they wallow in aloneness and refuse to take risks with
people.

Being with people is not always for the purpose of meeting
intimacy needs. Sometimes relationships can be used for an
escape. The question is whether or not you're afraid to be

alone with yourself. Having friends won't always be a buffer between you and loneliness. You may be lonely for a part of yourself that has not yet emerged. Being alone can provide an opportunity for you to tune into yourself. It can be a time to integrate new thoughts, ideas, and feelings. Integration of yourself doesn't take place on the run.

Unfortunately, most marriages haven't learned to tolerate the need for privacy. Only a mature relationship permits one partner the freedom to request time alone without the spouse interpreting it as rejection. Consequently, the excuse to be alone often comes after an argument. Unconsciously or consciously one sets up an argument in order to achieve physical and emotional distance. How much healthier the relationship would be if individuals could state the need to be alone, have it respected and regarded as natural, and then work together so that each person could have that need met.

As one man related, "My wife is hurt whenever I request time to myself. She accuses me of not loving her. Because her father never did anything without her mother being present, she assumes my need is unnatural and inappropriate. Yet I just want time to be alone to think. I wonder if she's crazy—or am I?"

Facing the Fears

Aloneness is not an issue just for those who are married. Often the need to be alone is smothered by intense emotional feelings. After a divorce or separation, solitude can be a painful reminder of the death of a relationship. Eventually, the fear of aloneness is replaced by the need for self-confrontation. The reorganization of life after a divorce or a death requires painful grief work which may take up to two years to complete. Hopefully, a person won't overreact to the fear of being alone and jump into a premature intimate relationship. Some hope it will be a cure-all, but it only postpones dealing with aloneness. Sooner or later, the pain will surface, and leave no way out but through it. The task of reorganizing life without one's mate requires periods of aloneness, which of necessity are painful. Facing the fears is the only way to learn to be autonomous.

As one woman replied, "I hate walking through my empty house. It just points out my need more vividly. But I know I can't constantly live in fear of going home. And I don't have the energy to plan activities every night of the week."

Being alone and lonely are not the same thing. Some people are so hemmed in by hectic schedules that when asked if they are ever lonely, they react with surprise. Often in amusement, they announce that they don't have time to be lonely. They might yearn for time alone, but loneliness is a feeling that evades them, perhaps. It could be that such persons use busyness as a way to avoid being present to themselves.

Look around you. Our society discourages introspection. No child was ever punished by sending him to be with a crowd of people. More often, it's "Go to your room." The message, loud and clear, is that aloneness is punishment and rejection. We live in a coupled world. Singles daily confront the image of family TV dinners, greeting cards from "both of us," and the team spirit. This is not to be critical of conformity or togetherness. Rather, it is to acknowledge that this is a society that frowns on aloneness even though people require some amount of privacy. Those without it are often more lonely than people who choose to create times of aloneness.

Obviously, the capacity to be alone varies from individual to individual. I have a friend who works every day and is busy every evening. Yet she's a very lonely individual. Another friend lives alone in a house but enjoys the solitude after a hectic day at her office. Some people feel loneliest when they're with their families during a holiday season. I've seen several families who've been together at Christmastime, but instead of feeling warm, they feel isolated, lonely, and cut off from themselves.

One woman described Christmas as "the most miserable day of my life. People are together pretending to be cheerful, but deep inside other feelings rumble around. The Christmas after my grandmother died, everyone pretended to be happy because Christmas is supposed to be merry. Yet, each of us missed this lady who had spent every Christmas with us for years. I felt so lonely, so fake. It would have been much easier if we could have talked about our sadness instead of pretending it away."

The circumstances of your life, your environment, your self-concept—so many variables influence your reactions to loneliness and aloneness. Beginning in childhood, you learn to adapt. How you handle crisis and isolation as an adult depends largely on how you responded as a child. You received messages then, just as you do now, on what intimacy and rejection mean, and how to handle unpleasant feelings. One professor of human development put it this way, "We wrongly assume that we'll grow out of childhood reactions. If you were angry and without a sense of humor as a child, don't expect adulthood to eliminate it. You'll probably mature into an angry, humorless 80-year-old. Age will merely make everything more pronounced! It boils down to this: if you were a crabby little brat at 10, you'll be an even crabbier old man or woman! We tend to "improve" our qualities with time.

An Appreciation of Aloneness

You *can* change behavior and attitudes, but often it's only through the result of a profound experience. Solitude can provide a timely opportunity to examine yourself and determine what you want to change. Solitude itself is *not* an answer; it's merely part of the process.

If a person had a sense of himself as a child, he will be better able to use times of aloneness constructively when he is an adult. It can be a time for creativity. It can even be a time when you enjoy your own company. However, an appreciation of aloneness doesn't occur overnight. It begins with your understanding the messages you received in your family. For instance, Jane, a woman in her 30s, recalled that her parents "disciplined" her by refusing to talk with her after she'd broken a family rule. If she were late from a date, she received the silent treatment from her parents. For Jane, being alone meant a form of silent rejection.

In another situation, Frank remembered that his family functioned under the motto of "peace at any price." He recalled occasions when he withdrew from the family in order to manage feelings of anger. Because he wasn't encouraged to communicate his feelings in a healthy way, he learned that unpleasant feelings were bad and not to be talked about. As an adult, he associates being alone with depression and unacceptable feelings. That was how he related as a child growing up. He turned anger in on himself. Consequently, he spent time alone, depressed.

Another man remembered his parents as encouragers. "They enjoyed time together as well as time alone. From their example, I learned that being alone doesn't mean rejection. It often is a choice and a productive use of time."

What messages did you receive in childhood? Rhonda, a woman in her early 20s, recalled what her mother said to her before she left for her freshman year at college. "I'm glad that you have the opportunity, but I dread being left alone." "Alone" meant desertion and responsibility for her mother's sadness. Today, Rhonda has graduated from college, and places the expectations of friends, co-workers, and family above her own. Even when she already has plans, she sacrifices them if someone needs her to do something else. The message of aloneness has been translated into guilt over using time to pursue personal interests.

A check with the parents of each of these individuals would probably reveal that their perception of family life was different from that of the child. It's important not to constantly blame parents. Most parents do the best they can, based on the messages they learned growing up in *their* families. Once you understand your own perception, blaming parents is merely a way to avoid assuming responsibility for your life. Discover the messages of your childhood as a way to begin to appreciate yourself in your times alone. Pigeonholing messages in right and wrong categories is inappropriate. Perceptions are real, not right or wrong. No value judgment is needed to justify your feelings.

By slowly converting your fears into an appreciation of solitude, you can use time with yourself to explore your questions. People frequently look restlessly for *answers* to the meaning of their lives, yet they search people, places, and books without first knowing what their *questions* are. One who has not made a friend of solitude wants answers immediately. In aloneness, you can pay attention to your innermost self and learn the questions of your life.

If you don't use aloneness productively, you become greedy for other people's answers. You become overly dependent, clinging, and explotive. You learn to use people for the fulfillment of your own wants and needs.

A Time for Learning

If aloneness can progressively become a time for learning what you already know, the capacity for relationships strengthened. Being related then involves a respect for individual needs, an awareness of the benefits of privacy, and at the same time, a greater capacity for intimacy. Aloneness can then be respected as an opportunity for growth.

It requires time. Converting overwhelming loneliness into times of solitude is a process of life. Often, it seems beyond one's grasp in days, weeks, or months of intense pain. But once solitude is experienced for the first time, the meaning it has for you will cause you to continue the search for it.

Solitude and alonencss. Only words, but the message behind them offers a deeper way to be related. Perhaps one of the most graphic analogies is in the meaning of friendship. At times I can see a friend clearer in his absence. Physical presence often gets in the way of the potential of a relationship. I might not see the inner beauty and character of a friend while with him because I am too busy protecting my own vulnerability. Distance provides aloneness to see past the barriers into the heart. It's a reminder that the relationship is a gift.

Solitude can provide a greater capacity to respond to others. Jesus didn't hesitate to withdraw from the crowds when He felt the need. He periodically departed from His disciples in order to be with Himself and pray to God. He provided the most important example of aloneness. Even when people didn't understand, He did what was needed to regain strength to meet the crowds (Luke 5:16). In solitude, He asked God the questions of His life. Never did He take a poll from His disciples, as we often do with friends, to make decisions. He claimed time to be alone, struggled within, and prayed.

Jesus lived a message for us. Having faith means involvement in life and take responsibility for choices. It means taking a stand, exposing oneself to life and to God. Faith doesn't prevent the need for aloneness. The person with faith may be more open to loneliness and aloneness by virtue of the demands made by God. Jesus achieved a balance—He was related to people and followed the will of His father. He also lived with moments of aloneness. How do *you* live aloneness?

Living Your Loneliness

During the day or week, respond to these questions from your own experience:

1. When do you need to be alone?
2. What message do you have from your introspection?
3. What expectations do you have for yourself that were born in your childhood?

5

Myths about Loneliness

The reality of loneliness is seldom debated, but the meaning it has for our lives is. The resolution of lonely times doesn't come in escaping or ignoring them, but in entertaining the questions that occur during the experience. Hopefully, an exploration of the common myths that surround loneliness will offer a perspective for reflection and dialogue.

Myth #1: Christians aren't lonely

Loneliness contains an element of pain in it that is intensified by your circumstances of life, how you relate to faith, and how people respond to you.

The importance of human response is evident in a story that was told by Rev. Dan Yeary. He traditionally concluded Sunday evening worship services by having the entire congregation sing the closing prayer. Members and visitors stood, held hands with the persons on both sides of them, and sang the benediction. During the course of opening his mail one day, Rev. Yeary read a letter from an elderly member of the congregation. It read: "Thank you for ending the service by having the congregation hold hands. I live a very lonely life and Sunday evening is the only time I'm touched by another person all week." This woman knew loneliness, and the pain of disregard. Living with depersonalization is difficult, and feeling unaccepted as a human being is even more painful. The outstretched hand of the person seated next to her made a difference to the woman who wrote the letter.

The relationship of loneliness and faith is evident throughout the Bible. Psalm 22 begins with, "My God, my God, why hast Thou forsaken me?" The believer is not immune from pain, but he has faith in God and His ultimate purpose. That context permits us to ask the important question, "Why?" You may know that God exists, but understanding His purpose and how He works is an entirely different matter. It is often easy to fall into the trap of thinking that faith is only answers with no room for questions. Faith helps you know what questions to ask, rather than leaving you to forsake God during times of personal anguish.

The question of the Psalmist comes from one in pain. Were it not for his faith, he would have no one to turn to, and if he weren't experiencing personal pain, questions about the meaning of life would go unasked. Life's meaning is found in living with the questions rather than trying to escape them.

Within the course of a year, a 35-year-old man attended funerals for his grandmother, his father, and his wife. His wife's fight with cancer occurred during a two-year period in which she seldom was free of pain. The man agonized through that last year, until finally, only he and his two-year-old daughter remained. James, a close friend, tried to comfort him, but he hadn't been acquainted with such grief in his own life. As the two men talked, James finally said, "I care about you. But the only one who really understands suffering and loneliness is God. Talk to Him."

James understood that all the talk you and I do about pain is merely academic until we are actually faced with living through the experience. Christ suffered for man, but He also suffered *with* man and *as* man. None of us is asked to undergo an ordeal as painful as the one Christ faced. He can comfort, for He personally understands. He's been there!

Psalm 22 is a process. It begins with cries and questions and concludes with praise. Moving through loneliness, or any type of pain, is not an answer in itself. Walking the road of faith and being open to the experiences of life, provides growth in Christian character.

Christians *do* experience loneliness and the questions that grow from it. Having faith doesn't imply you are immune to the stresses of life. Rather, it's a statement that you are open to whatever you must face, and that through faith you can grow from it. Unfortunately and inappropriately, people who judge by the standard, "Christians don't have problems or get lonely" miss the point completely. Faith offers the attitude and the strength for each person to face life head-on, including questions without simple answers.

Myth #2: Loneliness means failure and rejection

For many, self-image is dependent on *how others see you.* Rather than developing their unique inner resources, many people run from a clear picture of themselves. Being lonely has come to mean that "people don't want to be with you." If you question that, think about how many times people have said they were lonely, when asked the question, "How are you?" Rather than being viewed as a natural part of life, loneliness has been interpreted as rejection, and admission of it is shunned.

When the first pangs of loneliness are felt, people react as if they were confronting a catastrophe. How you cope with feelings of loneliness has to do with who defines you, and who decides your concept of success and failure. Often, it's your parents, peers, co-workers, anyone but yourself. Yet, the most important lessons you can learn no one can teach you. The battles must be fought within. Until you refuse to make others' expectations your prison, you will be tempted to run from a clearer picture of who you are.

Myth #3: If I work at it hard enough, I won't be lonely

Quite the contrary. If you go with the feelings and sink into your confusion, things become clearer than if you fight them. That's the beginning point for coordinating what you seem to be with what you are. Life is problem-solving rather than the absence of trouble. Running from loneliness, whether by over-eating, busyness, or whatever, only leaves you with lowered self-esteem. The only way out is through it; the only way that you can learn what you can become is to accept yourself and your feelings as they are.

Myth #4: Being with people will cure loneliness

Crowds, success, goals—none of them is a cure. Fill in your own statement, "When I'm _____ enough, I won't be lonely." Neither constant relatedness nor constant aloneness will cure loneliness. Use your lonely moments to explore your own limits and boundaries. Times of loneliness and pain can motivate you to take stock of yourself. If you know your limitations as well as your potential, then you're free to live with yourself realistically. Paradoxically, understanding the questions of limits frees you to explore and enjoy life in greater depth.

Myth #5: No one chooses to be lonely

Some people are more afraid of intimacy than they are of loneliness. Rather than take risks with people, they maintain a safe emotional distance. If you're in a relationship with such a person, the temptation would be to blame yourself and to conclude that something about you is unlovable. Yet the person's fear of love and intimacy is his or her problem to handle.

Try to accept that if a relationship doesn't grow, it doesn't

necessarily mean it's your responsibility. Attempt to understand the person and not interpret his inability to risk as a
rejection of you. Understanding, rather than critical judgment,
may be the first step toward his dropping the protective
barrier. Even if it isn't, it will aid you in understanding that
people are at different places in terms of their ability to be
involved in intimate relationships.

Myth #6: Changing my environment will cure loneliness

Within the last three years, one man has moved six times,
traded cars seven times, had three different jobs, and asks,
"Why am I so lonely?" Frequently, people blame the school,
town, job, church, government, or minister when they are
lonely and disillusioned. However, the responsibility for your
feelings is yours, and until you accept it, you'll make no prog-
ress toward living with yourself. Manipulation of the environment may offer a temporary respite from restlessness. A
change of scenery may offer excitement. But eventually problems will have to be faced. The moving cycle is no solution in
itself.

Myth #7: Only the introspective few do anything about loneliness

Everyone does something to ease loneliness pain. Some have
learned to face it, and learn from it. Others react to it by
various methods devised over the years. Employing manipu-
lative techniques learned in childhood, gossip, watching soap
operas, avoiding confrontation—the list is endless. Many use
up energy in nonproductive ways, trying to avoid facing themselves. As one woman remarked, "I ate myself into hopeless
despair. Whenever I felt lonely, I raced for the kitchen. I ate,
hungry or not, trying to ease the pain. Then I felt guilty and
fat! It became a never-ending cycle."

Another man echoed her pain. "I couldn't comfortably
spend time with myself. When I developed a case of the blahs,

I played a game. I called it "If Only" because I fantasized that if only something exciting happened, or someone new came into my life, then I'd feel good. A friend finally helped me when he interrupted my escape with one sentence, 'You're not running *to* anything,' he said. 'You're running *from* someone —yourself.' That scared me. Deep inside I knew that he was right, even though my first impulse was to be angry."

Everyone does something about loneliness; you choose how you will respond.

Myth #8: Marriage will solve loneliness

Numerous people marry, expecting marriage to eradicate loneliness. But people can be lonely in marriage, too, regardless of how healthy or unhealthy the marital relationship is. You don't develop an immunity to uncomfortable feelings with the wedding vow! This myth will be discussed more fully in the next chapter.

Myth #9: Singles are the loneliest of all people

Increasingly, singlehood is being accepted as a viable lifestyle. In addition, many are learning to look into their loneliness and grow from it. There are people who enjoy being single just as there are those who enjoy being married. And, many people wish they could change their marital status. However, being fully human is not measured in terms of marriage or singleness. Its meaning is found in becoming a whole person regardless of your life-style.

Myth #10: Children aren't lonely, just moody

Children begin separation from their parents at birth. From then on, they face a time of balancing increasing needs for independence with the desire for security. The messages about life, dealing with conflict, expressing verbal and physical affection, are received within the family. Children learn whether their feelings are accepted as valid, and whether they'll be punished if their thoughts are different from those of their parents. Reasonable discipline for *behavior* is a constructive act of love while punishment for *feeling* a certain way discounts the worth of the individual. Children often feel misunderstood, not only by parents and other adults, but also by themselves. Loneliness comes during self-evaluation and learning to assume responsibility for oneself. But it's also present during family crises, such as divorce or death experiences, and moving to another city. Helping a child deal with realities of family life facilitates his maturing process.

One woman explained, "I was protected from death as a child. I was never permitted to attend funerals, because my parents felt it would upset me. Now, I'm petrified of dying and of attending the funerals of relatives and friends. I didn't grow up with birth and death being a natural process of life."

Children have amazing resilience if they're permitted to face realities and are given explanations appropriate to their age. Even so, loneliness will be a part of their lives whether they verbally communicate it or not.

Loneliness is a reality of life. We have only to choose its meaning and trust the process.

Living Your Loneliness

During the day or week, respond to these questions from your own experience:

1. What are your questions about faith?

2. How do you view loneliness? What message about yourself does it convey?

6

All in the Family

The family is often expected to provide a shelter from loneliness. Yet families are already asked to withstand severe stresses in today's society. There aren't simple answers to such questions as: Are these unrealistic expectations imposed on the family and its members? Is it possible to alleviate some of the disillusionments of marriage? What roles do men and women play within marriage? What about the innumerable divorces today? What *is* a healthy marriage? If you're lonely in marriage, does that mean you have a bad marriage?

All kinds of loneliness are alive within the family. When a child is sick or in the hospital, the helpless loneliness can be overpowering. One couple described leaving their daughter's hospital room this way: "We kissed her good-night and shut the door to her room. Walking down the hospital corridor, we felt an agonizing numbness. Not being with our baby and having the nurse usher us out was frightening."

When a mate is out of town, or out of reach for the day, it can often be a lonely time. Missing someone, especially a person you love, arouses feelings that can't be resolved by filling your life with other people.

Growing pains are lonely times, and they occur throughout the life of a marriage. Yesterday's dreams can become today's illusions. Most couples are unprepared for the demands of marriage. Many couples planned the wedding to the last detail, assuming the ceremony was synonymous with being married. The marriage actually begins when the honeymoon ends!

People enter marriage in the bliss of ignorance, expecting inappropriate things from the relationship and from a mate. They begin with an image of marriage and a fantasy about what *they* want their mate to be like. To see the true image of your mate is a painful experience. To let someone see you real—your attitudes, fears, and dreams—can be just as threatening. Intimacy becomes too scary; anger either explodes or is suppressed. You're afraid to get to know each other as you really are and communication becomes merely sharing facts.

As one woman explained, "I thought marriage would be 'happy-ever-after-time.' That's the way it was on TV and in the movies. I expected marriage to take care of my problems and my insecurities. It only accented them."

Marriage is a growth process; not an answer, but a search. Only growing relationships can survive. And risking yourself with another is the only way to move beyond the wall of a superficial relationship. The greatest risk is not risking.

The problem of being alone and yearning for closeness and connectedness with another person begins at infancy. It continues throughout life and is evident in at least two important expectations with which people enter marriage. The first is that the relationship will be close and take care of any unresolved need. In courtship, this expectation is observed when two people play down the differentness between them, as if to say that closeness only occurs with conformity. The second expectation is the fantasy of what a good marriage is, and how one must behave in order to have a good marriage.

What Prevents a Loving Marriage?

Loneliness in marriage is heightened by the inability of a couple to deal with various aspects of the relationship. The question then becomes: What is it that prevents a healthy, warm, loving marriage? Current literature is full of "reasons." I'd like to offer several suggestions, not as answers, but as questions for you to pursue in thinking of your marriage or the marriage of your parents.

1. How do you deal with love and anger?
2. Can you appreciate differentness?
3. Do you communicate effectively?
4. Does the relationship allow you to continue your emotional growth?
5. Do you have a commitment to growth?

To experience life, you will have some degree of loneliness, pain, and fear. And if you don't learn to relate to people in your family in a healthy manner, loneliness and suffering are heightened. So the questions take on a new importance.

The quest for love that's seen in movies, novels, and advertising, is sometimes given the status of a cure-all for life's problems. What isn't mentioned is that to learn to love also involves learning to deal with anger. Christians sometimes view anger as a negative emotion. They cling to the gift of love in 1 Corinthians 13, but that's an *ideal* statement about love. As a human being, you must learn to live creatively with the tension between the *reality* of how you live and the *ideal,* which is a model. That tension requires that you use conflict creatively, rather than becoming depressed or suppressing angry feelings.

Alice, a woman in her mid-40s, told how she and her husband dealt with anger. "We had a game we played, although we never talked about the rules. One of us called attention to an issue that troubled us, and the other one debated the merits of the case. From there, each of us listed the shortcomings of the other from the history of our marriage.

By this time, the discussion was voiced in the key of loud! Whoever tired first ended the discussion. My husband cut off dialogue by working in his workroom for an hour or so. Whenever I tired first, I stared out the window in silence. He got the message! Whatever the original issue was got lost in the shuffle.

"The effect on our children was quite revealing. Neither of our daughters openly expresses anger, not to me nor to each other. I worry about how they'll relate when they become adults."

In some circles, there has been such an emphasis on expressing anger that venting it has been made the ideal. Exploding in anger is not a solution; that's merely dumping extra baggage onto your mate. Once you recognize your anger, try to determine what triggered it. Then, acknowledge the feelings to your mate, and refrain from verbal attacks or sniping with snide remarks. This is an important step toward a constructive marriage relationship, because you claim the discomfort while stating that you'd like to work through it. As the two of you examine what has happened, attempt to understand what created the anger and what options are available to resolve it. Claiming anger and working through it *with* your mate rather than exploding, can provide insight into where your relationship can grow.

Work and some amount of time are required to learn to deal with love and anger. People who have suppressed anger for years will have to learn to vent it as part of their own work with themselves. Having a professional third party to aid you on the journey is helpful. Learning to deal constructively with anger in a love relationship requires a commitment that both people will do so, and the ability to forgive again and again and again. Your relationship already has patterns for dealing (or not dealing) with conflict, which will be hard to change. Being willing to work on the relationship is the first step in what is a *process* of relating. Conflict is a healthy sign. Any number of things could cause problems in marriages simply because people don't care enough to deal with them. When you really love someone, you face the problems that are a natural part of being intimately related. Where there is love, there is anger; where there is intimacy, there is differentness.

Curiosity, Not Condemnation

One man described his marriage relationship as impossible. "I just don't understand it," he said. "The things I liked about Karen before we were married bug me now. And things I *thought* we had in common, we don't! I expected her to meet all my needs, and even that's disappointing. I used to think she was my better half. Now I'm not so sure!"

This fellow was in touch with the fact that courtship is a time of maximum dishonesty. People see, hear, and believe what they want to during a dating relationship. The first awareness that your mate and the image in your head are not the same can be disappointing. Yet this *can* be another step toward a maturing relationship. Rather than condemning differentness, be curious about it. *How* and *what* your mate thinks are the important questions instead of *why* he or she feels a certain way. Find out *how* a certain decision was made instead of asking, *"Why* did you do it *that* way?"

The courtship of two emotionally fused people becomes a marriage, and offers an opportunity for individuation. You can get to know each other as you are. Hopefully, the marriage will be open enough to allow each of you the opportunity to master the continuing developmental stages of life.

As you deal with the marriage relationship, you'll discover that your mate can't meet all of your needs. Nor is that a realistic expectation. If six out of 10 of them can be met, that's a time for celebration. Determine what your needs are, and talk about the ones the marriage can meet. Explore how the other needs can be met on a realistic basis. Perhaps the two of you can periodically examine your expectations for the marital relationship.

Learning to communicate with each other about the relationship offers a growing edge of support, intimacy, and an appreciation of each other. Assume that the relationship will change, and that change isn't necessarily a bad word. How you relate in your first year of marriage won't provide what you need as individuals in your 30s, 40s, 50s, and beyond. Hopefully, your relationship will reflect your growth in its own maturity.

Learning to Communicate

Communication is the key, but it works only if both people are committed to it. Numerous books explain the art of communication. No one has it mastered nor will anyone ever master it. But here are five overly simplistic beginnings:

Listen. Try to hear what the other person is saying and not saying. What are the nonverbal messages? Very few people have had someone in their lives who would listen to their hopes and dreams and feelings. Consequently, they spend time trying to get what they never had, and in the process, don't ever *give* the gift of hearing another person. Even parents sometimes tell their children what they are to become without ever *hearing* and *helping* them to discover what direction God wants them to take.

Learn to request. Most people make requests by complaining. They are more likely to gripe, "Why don't you stay home more?" than say, "I'd like to be with you more often."

Try to respond with what you're really feeling. Integrity of feelings is the art of being real with another person. This may be the most painful struggle of all. It begins when you learn how to listen to yourself.

Develop a sense of humor about yourself. Not as a way to avoid dealing with issues, but as a companion along the journey.

Learn what Christian marriage is. A Christian marriage can be described as the union of two individuals who have faith in God, and enough faith in themselves to risk sharing their humanness.

As you grow, your whole philosophy will be translated through actions to your children, if you have any. Children are not a possession, they're a gift. They're not little adults, but growing individuals whose education about families is born in yours.

To be a Christian in a loving family doesn't mean, as the song says, never having to say, "I'm sorry." Rather, it means saying, "I'm sorry," over and over again. The best gift you can give yourself is acceptance of who you are and encouragement to grow. The other side of the same coin is being able to make mistakes and learn from them, where you can be human and learn about love and anger and creative conflict, where you can experience interdependence with family members while you test your wings of independence with the rest of the world. Loneliness then becomes manageable and silence not so deafening.

The key lies in the ability to give and receive forgiveness, and the capacity to express appreciation (Matt. 6:9-14).

Neither age nor success nor public acclaim removes the need to be affirmed. In fact, success as a goal in itself is empty and lonely. If you are unwilling or unable to express gratitude and love to your mate, consider why. What's scary about risking closeness?

Expressing appreciation begins with affirming the gifts that the *other person* has to contribute. As you can, thank your mate for specific contributions made to the relationship and to you. Most people are well-versed in handling criticism, but embarrassingly shy about receiving affirmation. Yet it's those tender words that they daydream about in their lonely moments.

The really meaningful lessons and the hardest problems

never get solved once and for all. You begin by listening, and continue doing more of the same, as the listening teaches you how to listen.

Loneliness in families and in marriage is natural. But it grows in proportion to how *little* attention we give to the personal relationships in our families. Healthy marriages grow from reevaluating expectations, learning new skills, accepting conflict as natural and learning to profit from it, and taking positive steps to enhance family life through the church, and through whatever marital enrichment aids are necessary.

You may think of the typical family as the two adults and two children viewed in family albums. However, on entering the final quarter of the 20th century, more diverse family forms are evident. Currently, the nuclear family, two adults and their children, comprise 44% of the United States' population. The other 56% is made up of various other family units.

While there's loneliness in marriage, especially if there's no real sharing and communication, there are lonely times in these other family forms. Loneliness is a theme with single adults, in one-parent families, with couples who are childless, in roommate families, in blended families, and in the empty nest when the children are gone.

Without an intimate relationship, the risk of emotional isolation soars. It's this situation which accentuates the sense of loneliness.

Widowed Adults

John and Nelle are both widowed, and each has found the adjustment difficult. As I talked with them, each explained that loneliness is a major problem.

"I remember so well the day of the funeral," Nelle sighed. "At first it was like moving through a fog. The minutes dragged by—each one seemed like an hour. Relatives had come from out of town; friends were swarming around; and I was in a state of shock. A few weeks later, the reality of Ed's death hit me. I felt dizzy and burdened down by the loss.

"Everywhere were memories: Ed's voice, his laugh, even his temper played through my mind. I cried until I made myself physically sick. Sometimes I'd wander from room to room knowing he was gone, but hoping it was all a bad dream. I remember how startled I was to look at the calendar and realize that it hadn't been days since the funeral; weeks and months had drifted by. I could scarcely realize that huge blocks of time were gone. Death is permanent. Loneliness had been my companion during those weeping days. Ed could visit only in my imagination. There was no use searching the house for a memory."

John replied to Nelle's memories. "I understand what you mean. I feel such a void without my wife. Something will happen during the day, and I'll think, 'Oh, I must remember to tell . . .' and there isn't anyone to share it with when I get home. It's especially lonely at night. The only sounds in the house are the ones that I make. We didn't do a lot socially, but at least we had each other. Now, it's so empty. There's no need for me to organize my out-of-town trips around Janice anymore. I miss that."

Both Nelle and John felt a kind of loneliness that they called homesickness. They missed the life-style they'd had with their mates. No longer is it couples' golf, parties, or dinners.

For others, social relations may be altered during long illnesses. Some people report that they didn't realize how isolated they'd become until their mate died. Their social relationships withered away over a gradual lapse of time, and they felt awkward trying to reenter the friendship circle.

One woman described her feelings of loneliness this way, "I feel like a fifth wheel when I'm with old friends. On occasion, I stifle my tears because crying in public makes people ill at ease. I guess self-control is more valued than being real.

I feel like I make interactions difficult just by my presence. So I withdraw."

Loneliness as a result of decreased involvement with friends is common. Whether it's due to changed relationships, reduced income, moving to a new neighborhood, or for some other reason, the lack of intimacy can be painful.

However, not everyone is deeply lonely after the death of a mate. One woman described her feelings. "I grew up without brothers and sisters, so I've always been accustomed to being alone and entertaining myself. I guess I learned to enjoy my own company. I don't mean that I don't like people; it's just that being alone doesn't devastate me. Even before my husband's death, I spent time alone periodically."

Another widow had a closely knit extended family. Interaction with people she loved helped her to move forward and not wallow in lonely pity. Marlene, a woman in her mid-50s, said she felt relieved after her husband died. "At least, I won't have to live with his alcoholism every day," she said.

When asked what advice they'd give to new widows and widowers, John and Nelle immediately said, "Keep busy." Recent widows usually are busy for the sake of activity. Later, however, activities are chosen for their meaning to the individual. Busyness without meaning may be no more than an attempt to avoid the anxiety of loneliness.

Beyond activity, however, is the need for significant relationships. Getting to know different types of people can help your reentry into life, even if you have to push a little to make yourself do it.

The most severe loneliness may come during those moments which remind you of your mate. John recalled that the hardest times were Christmas, birthdays, and in July when they used to visit his wife's parents on their vacation. Slowly, with time, he was able to survive those periods without despairing. He felt emotionally freer and able to release his continual mourning.

Little is known about the process of giving up a former mate. Individual differences influence how long you're "married" to the husband or wife who died. Some seem to hold on to the deceased spouse for years, perhaps forever. Others feel free within a year or so to consider another marital relationship. However, the former marriage isn't forgotten with another attachment. It underscores the reality that major losses, like death, do not become an emotional fact overnight.

Divorce or Separation

The grief process that accompanies a death experience, of which loneliness is a part, is similar to what occurs in divorce or separation. Of all the feelings of the newly separated, loneliness is perhaps the most important. For some, it's a guard against vulnerability. After a recent separation, contact with other people can be painful and threatening. Solitude becomes a treasured friend that protects against premature relationships. For the majority of people in this situation, however, loneliness is a gnawing, recurring pain that follows them everywhere. They grasp for the telephone or books or people —anything that looks like a life preserver. In desperate moments, being in touch with another person offers no immediate solution, but may make them feel less alone. In fact, the physical presence of a friend or family member may be the only real antidote. Knowing they will be with someone later in the day helps to ease the blackness of the mood.

However, the formerly married person soon discovers that coupled friends seldom know how to be helpful. If you're relieved that the marriage is over, they question how you can find pleasure in such a situation. It triggers shock, alarm, even criticism from your friends. They say it would be easier to forgive you if you were miserable. Yet, if you cry, vent your anger, or talk about feelings of guilt, friends tend to withdraw. You seldom know the meaning of the divorce to your friends. And watching them choose sides between you and your former mate, or completely retreat from you, or turn a deaf ear to your pain only increases your loneliness. Eventually, the gulf between you may widen as you develop new friends that are compatible with your life-style. But this will require time and emotional energy.

For a long time, churches have struggled to uphold the ideal of marriage as stated in the Bible. But increasingly, marriages of Christians are dying. For whatever reasons, divorce has become more prevalent. The tension of upholding the ideal but living with the reality has caused many pastors to rethink their condemnation of people who were formerly married. Like it or not, divorce is a fact in many lives. Meeting people at their point of pain is more the message of Christ than is sitting in self-righteous judgment.

I'm reminded of a singles' conference held in a West Texas city in which a woman called and asked, "I'm newly divorced and heard your church is having a conference. Are *you* sure it's OK for me to come?" The minister who answered the call said, "Of course, you can come. We'd love to have you." The tragedy is that the question even had to be asked. The loneliness of the divorce process is demanding; the rejection by those who could offer support is devastating. This particular minister must have understood the God of the second chance and what resurrection meant!

Divorce and after can be a difficult time. For some, it's a growing experience that teaches how to let go and trust God.

Those Who Never Marry

The never-married form another category of singleness. Whether single by choice or circumstances, loneliness in some form is a partner. Usually, being lonely motivates people to define or integrate a *new* relationship; in essence it drives them to other people. Loneliness can be a response to the absence of a close, intimate relationship. In such cases, social activity is not a cure-all.

However, those who never marry are at a *different* point than are those who suddenly face the somersault emotions of death or divorce. Over the years, the unmarried develop patterns of relationships and aloneness. They aren't suddenly removed from a secure, happy or unhappy, status quo. Their world is familiar, and they don't depend on previous couples' relationships for support.

Yet, singles must deal with the expectations they have for their life. If they wanted to marry, and didn't, they can face heavy disappointment. Patricia, a single woman, described her experience to me.

"I grew up thinking I'd go to college and marry after my senior year. But the time came and passed by. I felt rejected, a failure. After all, my parents sent me to college to get two things, a degree and a husband, and in that order! I've had some good relationships since then, but there hasn't been anyone I've wanted to spend my life with. I've had a couple of serious opportunities to marry, and nearly jumped at the chance with one guy, but decided against it. That was a scary, lonely time for me. What if no one else asked me? Would this be my last chance? All kinds of questions plagued me with doubts. I finally decided that marriage to the right partner would be OK; anything less than that was unthinkable."

I asked Patricia how she lived with her lonely times, and she told me that she began to face her life as she found it each day. "Sure, I get lonely," she explained. "But, I'm not going to postpone living today while I search for tomorrow. If I marry, it will be my choice, not as a trade-off for trumped-up security."

Patricia discovered that being uniquely human and whole was not dependent on her marital status. It had more to do with her own self-esteem and worth as a person.

Singles—widowed, divorced, separated, and never married —make friends their family. They are part of the community of a church and constitute part of that family. Some people have roommates who provide a sense of belonging. Gwen and Vicki have shared an apartment for a year. When asked how they decided to live together, Gwen replied, "Well, one day I realized that I was lonely for companionship. I like my privacy and, honestly, there are times when I enjoy just being with myself alone. But, I also had moments when I'd think that living with someone would have merits."

"Yeah," echoed Vicki. "I felt the same way. Only I hadn't had much luck with roommates. So I shied away from the idea. But going to a dark, empty apartment every day had its disadvantages. There was never anyone to share a funny or happy or sad moment with. That is, unless I called a friend on the telephone or made an effort to visit someone."

Gwen interrupted with, "I liked Vicki the first time I met her, but I didn't want to jump into a roommate situation until we'd formed a friendship."

"I think both of us were more comfortable about sharing an apartment after we'd gotten to know each other," Vicki said.

"I certainly couldn't do like a friend of mine does," Gwen laughed. "She advertises for a roommate in the city newspaper!"

Both women agreed that having a roommate helped ease the empty loneliness of feeling as if no one knows them very well.

"It's nice to feel understood," was how they described their unique "family" unit. They have separate social lives, although they occasionally host parties together. And they attend the same church, which creates a mutual spiritual interest. Gwen summed up her original loneliness this way:

"Having a roommate has helped ease the pain of not having a family nearby. My parents live in another city and my sister in another state. I live a full life, yet don't feel as self-centered as I did when I lived alone. It's great to share with another adult, yet still take responsibility for my own life. I haven't experienced intense loneliness in a long time."

Empty Nest Family

After a lifetime of raising children, the elderly spend their later years either alone or with their mate. Unfortunately, these times of potential fulfillment are often overshadowed by neglect. A great deal has been written about how the elderly suffer in isolation, cut off from others. The time has come to recognize that everyone suffers from being cut off from them!

Loneliness is prevalent among "senior citizens," primarily because mandatory retirement has become synonymous with having no place in life. Those with vitality haven't bought into the myth that "old age is a disease." Instead, they have a continued goal and a way of being useful. A kind of energy cuts through loneliness when you can affirm that you have a place.

One man volunteered how he combated our "throw-away" society. "I reviewed my whole life history," he said, "and I discovered that many of the experiences I'd had could be useful. Especially with the renewed interest in "roots," I learned a new way of contributing. I've been invited to give an oral history course at my church to children of elementary school age. It will be quite exciting to talk about their heritage in terms of experiences I've had!"

This fellow is, unfortunately, the exception. Too many think "old" means unnecessary and unused. Another woman, a widow in her 70s, talked about her lonely moments. "For me, loneliness is a seldom occurrence. When my husband died, I was left with this huge house. I really didn't want to move nor did I want to live with my children. They have their own lives to live and as long as I can care for myself, I want to. Anyway, I don't want anyone to treat me like a dependent child. So I rented some of my rooms to four college kids. They were struggling through school and needed a place to stay, and I'm on a fixed income. So they pay modest rent, and we share in the cooking. When we can, we eat together and we get to know each other's friends. It's marvelous! It's easier to have an extended family with people who aren't your real family. You don't get caught up in an emotional tug-of-war. These college kids are really stimulating, and I think I have something to offer them in return."

What is missed by isolating the elderly is what comes with the wisdom of age. Not nostalgia or a return to the good old days, some of which weren't so good; rather, the elderly offer wisdom that only experience can teach. The last years of life can be the prime time for investigating the ultimate meaning of life. But so little discussion centers around a theology that stresses the values and significance of aging.

We assume that God is old, and that His wisdom represents the ages, but what about a theology of aging?

Not everyone has the extended families of the people mentioned above. Over half of the elderly are single and alone. Some have friends; others do not. Some can travel to visit relatives; others are too impoverished even to take a bus to a friend's house. Those who are not widowed may be confined to their homes. They've seen their neighbors die or move away, their ministers called to other churches, and their friends become physically ill.

Loneliness is accented in the life-styles of the elderly. Being old means different things to different people. How someone living beyond retirement is treated is a large factor in the blanket of loneliness that covers so many. Just look at the plight of some of those who have survived generations. The elderly know what it is to see their meager pensions and savings buy less and less. They know the loneliness of forced isolation as cars become too costly to maintain or too difficult to handle. They wait for family too busy to visit, for a bus that doesn't come, for a doctor who won't make house calls, for the day they lose more independence through disease, illness, or inability to move around.

For many, being old means nursing homes if they live in the city, and isolation if they live in a rural area. And for many, being elderly is being forgotten, except during election time. It's a time when they may not be touched by another human being, and that results in being imprisoned by loneliness.

Yes, many of the elderly are lonely and are treated like second-class citizens. Yet, the elderly, just as the young and middle-aged, want independence. Help, yes, but only when it's needed and not a fostering of patriarchal dependence just because age has signaled forced retirement from careers.

Becoming old is a transitional period in which you face, and must adapt to, disruptive changes. Certainly, if you're active, well-adjusted, and confident during mid-life, you'll carry those characteristics with you. But, you still have losses to deal with. For one thing, you're forced to retire from the work role that has added focus to your life. Even if your skills and ability are unchanged, you're separated from the mainstream of society and labeled "dependent."

As one man tearfully recalled, "All of a sudden I was a has-been. I got my gold watch and was turned away. Not having meaningful work has dampened my zest for living. There's no way to maintain self-esteem when one day I'm a productive engineer, and the next day I sit on my back porch and chase blue jays from the garden. I feel like I'm just waiting to die, or everyone else is, at least!"

The elderly person's self-image is affected by multiple losses of role, status, income, and health. And, as friends, family, and neighbors die or move, they discover that they're isolated at a time when they need emotional support. The fear and loneliness of such a plight often encourages withdrawal from community activities, which in turn increases isolation. Being caught in this cycle is a troublesome problem for numerous people.

Yet even the healthy and energetic must fight the stereotypes. In a society that rewards and is built for the young, many live with insensitivity toward the people whose ingenuity built this country. The fact is, many elderly people are capable of work, intellectual growth, and creative use of leisure time. You wouldn't think that was the case, however. Just look at advertising which focuses on the elderly; it centers around people unable to perform on their own behalf. The advertising reflects the mainstream public image we have of elderly people.

The elderly make up a large segment of American society. Many live in "rest homes." (Again, the subtle stereotype that the elderly spend their last days unproductively!) They eat together, share, fight, and talk as a family unit. Yet, another family form places the elderly, middle-aged, and the young together. This form is the church. The elderly generally place a high priority on relationships, regardless of age. Children and teenagers are valued as much as adults. Couples, the elderly, single-parent families, blended families (where two divorced or widowed partners have married each other), and traditional families are represented. The "family of faith" can provide a community to minister during turning points.

Have you ever walked along the beach and flirted with the waves? The waves wash gently against your feet until all of a sudden, a big wave splashes you up to your knees. These waves hit everyone at some time in their lives, usually when they're the most vulnerable. In this age of mobility, it's as if people have portable roots. Families often become those closest in proximity, whether they're relatives or not. With advancing age and changing circumstances, both the horizon of birth and the horizon of death come into clearer view. Whether you like it or not, you have to be involved with reevaluation. You assess the life you've already lived and consider the choices available for the next part.

Families won't protect you from loneliness, but they can provide support as each one weathers it. Take a lesson from Jesus, whose family was the disciples. Look around you. Who is your family and who are you inviting to become members of it?

Living Your Loneliness

During the day or week, respond to these questions from your own family experience.

1. Traditional family

a. What are some of the loneliest times you've encountered? (During a child's illness; when expectations were unrealistic, etc.)

b. What are aspects of your marital relationship that you have trouble dealing with? How do you plan to work on them?

c. How are you and your mate different? List viewpoints, ways of dealing with conflict, etc. Are you learning to appreciate the differentness?

d. What do you do with your anger? Do you make it a constructive or a destructive experience?

e. When was the last time you were angry with your spouse? A child? How did you deal with it? How would you do it differently?

f. What needs does your spouse meet? Can you celebrate those needs met, or do you major on the unmet needs? (Are some of your unmet needs unrealistic for a mate to meet?)

g. If your marriage is not what you'd like for it to be, how will you work on it? Will you seek professional counseling? Why or why not? Investigate what's available in your community and church to enrich your family life.

h. Identify your personal and relational goals in these areas: spiritual; mental; physical; emotional.

2. Single adults

a. List those people closest to you.

b. What steps are you taking to deal with loneliness?

c. List three goals for yourself in each of the following areas and set for yourself a definite time by which to achieve them: spiritual goals; mental goals; physical goals; emotional goals.

d. What times are most difficult for you? How do you deal with them?

3. Retired and Elderly

a. What are advantages of your age and life-style? Disadvantages?

b. Who is your family? Name them. They may be friends, relatives, neighbors, etc.

c. What things do you do to take care of yourself?

d. What is available in your community for you? If you don't know, call your minister and ask him.

e. Looking back over your life, think of those times or experiences that you can give to someone as an oral history.

f. What do you dislike about the stereotypes given to the elderly?

g. What are your goals for living? You're still a useful human being, you know!

4. Family of faith.

a. What programs are already set up in your church for families?

b. What are the growing edges, the areas that need more attention? (singles, elderly, marriage, etc.)

c. Do you condemn those "family units" which are not like yours? If so, why? Have you learned how to accept people for what they are?

d. What is your theology of aging? Everyone is aging, ready or not!

e. List your goals toward involvement in your local church. How do you plan to contribute?

f. Is church made up of people or programs? Think about it. What is the distinction, if any?

g. What examples of loneliness have you seen in your church?

7

The Company You Keep

The scene was a university cafeteria. People who were finished with their meals looked through the walls of glass that separated them from the outside. Eyes were focused on a favorite pastime, people watching. Students, loaded with books, walked up the stairs that were the only access from the underground cafeteria to the ground floor above. Several people passed the people-watchers with their eyes fixed on the stairs 10 yards away. No words were exchanged. Occasionally, people walked alone, unsurrounded by crowds.

Then appeared a girl with a cane, slowly making her way to the stairs. She moved haltingly, while the cane tested each step. Because of the structure of the staircase, students walked up the first 15 steps, zigzagged horizontally, then walked up the next 15 steps to the ground level. If you didn't make the horizontal sidesteps, you unavoidably walked back down to the underground level. It became obvious that the blind girl hadn't previously negotiated this particular staircase. She made the first set of stairs, but as she reached the landing she took steps forward instead of sideways. It was like climbing a ladder, reaching the top, and stepping down the rungs on the other side. The blind girl was again on the underground pavilion. She stood there for a moment, confused, then slowly circled back to the original steps to begin her climb again. She was literally walking in circles. The people-watchers sat motionless, without conversing. No attempt was made to reach out to the blind girl with the cane. In fact, no one moved as she repeated the same exercise in futility again.

On her third trip around, one of the people-watchers fumbled uncomfortably with his books. Quietly, he gathered his papers, pushed in his chair, and headed for the door. He moved from behind the protective glass wall that separated the people-watchers from the passersby on the other side. He quickly reached the girl, gently touched her arm, and received her smile. He guided her up both flights of stairs, while the people-watchers strained their necks to watch. The two of them smiled and parted. He'd cared enough to become involved with another person. The people-watchers returned to their task, gazing silently, uninvolved with each other or those walking by them.

One of the messages that appears throughout Jesus' ministry is His involvement with people. There are graphic lessons about how He related to significant people in His life, and how these people responded to Him. He chose twelve ordinary men to become His disciples. These men with their characters, their problems, their questions, and their backgrounds were chosen by Jesus to be His companions and to share the future of His ministry. The disciples exhibited traits that are part of intimate relating: love, friendship, jealousy, power struggles, betrayal, compassion, misunderstanding, skepticism. It's really a statement of a current bumper sticker: "Christians are not perfect people; just forgiven." Being human didn't nullify the uniqueness and gifts of each disciple. And apparently, Jesus didn't view diversity as a problem. Christ appreciated uniqueness and its opportunities.

One of the paradoxes of this social culture is that people

live closely together without meeting. The story of the blind girl is a commentary on how walls, even glass ones, serve to isolate people from involvement.

As a beginning in exploring relationships, look closer into the way Christ related to His "support system," the disciples. As He chose them, He began telling them who He was. Over the course of His ministry, He continually told them who He was, in different ways. As with all beginning relationships, there was curiosity, and there were questions and misinterpretations. The anguish of not being understood must have been a lonely experience at times. But Jesus always gave those around Him the freedom to be themselves, even when it was painful.

The disciples couldn't protect Jesus from going through the experiences He faced. Conversely, He didn't protect them from facing themselves and growing in faith and in their relationships with others.

He even gave the freedom for a relationship to deteriorate. Judas didn't understand what "Messiah" meant. Too late he understood that he didn't understand at all. Even when Jesus confronted him with future betrayal, Judas was able to respond to their relationship in his own way. What a poignant example of relationships changing!

Jesus understood that people have different things to offer in relationships. There were some who offered Him hospitality, others compassion; still others offered Him a retreat from the crowds.

People responded to Jesus in their own way, and met various kinds of needs. Even the Resurrection was met with the uniqueness of the individual. Mary recognized His voice when she thought He was the gardener at the tomb. She uttered the first sermon when she said, "I have seen the Lord" (John 20:14-18). John recognized His unique ability to catch fish when, at first, he thought Him to be just another fisherman (John 21:4-7). Peter, the Rock, was not always one of such strength. He'd denied Christ three times, but the Lord of the second chance confronted him face-to-face with love, and offered the same invitation of earlier years: "Peter, follow me" (John 21:15-19).

Thomas, the doubter, responded to the Resurrection with a question. He wasn't certain Christ had risen. He didn't look at faith as an alternative to knowledge, but as an avenue to wisdom. He wanted to see for himself. His doubt became a deeper commitment and truth as he openly confronted his questions.

Jesus experienced diversity in relationships, and appeared to value it. "He appeared also to me" was the message of Resurrection that described what happened in the lives of people. It also marked a time of saying good-bye. Christ could have risen, made His appearance known, and departed, but He didn't. He talked with those He'd been close to, explained what "good-bye" meant, and set the course for new directions "In His Name."

Relationships are important but they don't remain status quo for long. They grow, change, and adapt, but first there is involvement. Implications are there for modern readers, not only in faith, but also in how to relate to people. Who are *your* people?

Reams of material have been written about marriage, the single life, male-female relationships, teacher-student roles, and other interactions. Only recently have authors explored the patterns of relating and the significance of friends. Friendships reveal much about who you are, even some things you've hidden from yourself. Healthy relationships provide the backdrop and support system for you to deal with everyday realities. Destructive or stagnant relationships accentuate loneliness, whether you're married, divorced, widowed, or single. Learning how you relate not only can open up new insights into yourself, but also can pave the way for changes and creative friendships. One of the keys to your self-image can be discovered by looking at how you develop, or don't develop, meaningful friendship relationships.

Jessica, an attractive, slim woman in her mid-30s, recalled a painful lesson she'd learned about herself. "I grew up allowing people to take advantage of me. I seldom, if ever, said no to anyone, whether I wanted to or not. If a friend wanted to borrow something, fine. If someone wanted me to help them move, I'd change my plans to fit the schedule. Many nights I sat up listening to people detail their problems, yet never revealed myself. I didn't feel good about myself unless people were leaning on me.

"Eventually, I became depressed, and was unable to pull out of it. I talked to my minister, a sensitive man, who had professional training in understanding human behavior. I told him how lonely I was, how demanding people were of me. Through the course of our sessions, I tried to dump my problems on him, just as my friends did with me. An interesting thing happened though. He refused to take it! I was stunned. That was the only way I knew how to relate. I'm now in the process of examining the reality of my life!"

Jessica's problems are very common. She learned to relate by taking care of people. She got her needs met by mothering and nurturing other people. So Jessica selected friends who were dependent and would make demands on her. Until she learns to feel good about herself without having to "help" people, she'll remain lonely, disappointed, and depressed. For when she has a crisis in her life, these friends will be unable to offer her any emotional support. That's not the way the relationships with Jessica are set up.

Consequently, the friends that surround her will only reinforce her already low self-image. Part of what Jessica is learning is that she contributes to her poor self-esteem by her choice of friends. As she deals with her fear of trusting people, she'll be able to alter the destructive pattern of relating.

Relationships are affected by the picture you have of yourself. Do you think you're worthwhile? Do you accept your feelings as being OK? Do you care about you? Sometimes, Christians feel that thinking well of yourself is selfish or conceited. But an ego trip is different than a genuine appreciation of your own worth as a human being. Without the capacity to like yourself, you reinforce mistrust, fear, and loneliness.

It begins with who you are to yourself. Offering love and acceptance to others occurs only when you can do that for yourself. To the extent that you value yourself and your uniqueness, you can encourage others to do the same. The Bible undergirds this sense of worth. "Thou shalt love thy neighbor as thyself" assumes you value yourself.

Self-awareness is difficult. Most people are adept at side-stepping questions that create confrontations with themselves. They become accomplished at filling their lives with diversions, and masters at keeping people at arm's length. It increases their loneliness, and it uses up the energy they need to look inward.

Growth begins when you accept your limitations. You can't be all things to all people any more than you can be perfect. Where are your limits and in what areas? Naturally, maturity isn't a private matter. Growth occurs by exposing yourself to other persons, ideas, and feelings, and being open to their lessons. Listen to your feelings as you respond to others, especially to the significant people in your life. The tension of examining yourself calls you to move forward and creates an openness for God to work in your life.

At this point in your life, you may have many that you call friends or only a few. The quantity isn't important, but the *quality* of the relationship is.

Sandi

"When I divorced, the most unexpected thing I faced was how it affected my friends. The divorce came as a surprise to most people. Only one friend knew of the problems we'd had. Most of our couple friends have chosen sides in spite of our pleas that they not. The few couples who continue to relate to us both have their own set of problems. One couple can't seem to view us as individuals. They still relate to a couple. Bob and Shirley have tried to be understanding, but they wonder which of us to invite to what dinner party. I'm trying to meet other people who share some of my concerns, but it's difficult. Even with the singles' group at church, I find myself afraid to trust, yet too willing to meet other people's expectations.

"I'm so lonely. I feel caught in a transition. I want to learn to stand on my own two feet, but I desperately need someone to be a friend. I didn't realize how important friends were until my life became a whirlwind of emotions and events."

Fred and Judith

This couple is surrounded by people, but lonely. Fred's relationships are primarily business or golf associations. Judith plans the social calendar, which Fred both appreciates and resents. He doesn't like the friends Judith chooses; she tires of the wives of his business colleagues. Fred doesn't trust too many people. He's well liked because he's outgoing, concerned about others, and able to engage people in conversations. He has a powerful position in the company, is attracted to others with power, and he attracts those who sense power in him. But Fred is a complicated man. He knows more about his friends than they do about him. Self-disclosure is a liability as far as he's concerned. Occasionally, he has time in which to face himself, but not liking what he sees, his insecurity motivates him to chair more committees, attend more meetings, or agree to teach a Sunday School class for another year.

John and Eileen

One couple learned that friends are like an extended family. When their child was killed in an accident, friends responded with Christian concern and compassion. They'd always maintained friends that were couples, but each also had individual friends. After the death of their son, they needed these friends more than ever. They deeply grieved over Rob's death. During the part of the grief process when they angrily asked, "Why?" and questioned God's place in the tragedy, some acquaintances added to their grief. The people on the periphery of their lives said, "It was God's will," or, "This wouldn't have happened unless your faith has slipped. Has it?"

Not up to fighting such phrases, John and Eileen withdrew. They continued to attend church. They needed the strength God could give them more than ever. But they didn't reveal their anger to just anyone who asked, "How are you?" They were afraid some church members would think something was wrong in their spiritual lives, and they had all they could handle from people who meant well. They turned to their extended family of understanding friends when they wanted to be real. These people knew them well and understood their sorrow. They didn't rush in to fix anything. And they could be with them "In His Name" without preaching a sermon or checking up on their faith.

Qualities of Relationship

These excerpts provide a glimmer of the importance of friendship. One of the basic needs of all people is to love and be loved. Without it, loneliness and its effects on self-esteem are devastating.

But certain qualities in relationships, if not met, can enhance feelings of alienation and loneliness anxiety.

Expectations. You enter relationships with all kinds of nonverbal expectations: what the relationship will be like, what you believe constitutes a good friend, and how you want a friend to respond. Often you may assume you know your friend's needs and limitations, and what he wants from you, without checking it out with him. For example, a friend tells you about a personal crisis in his life. You rush in to give advice or tell him what you'd do if it were you (which you *can't* know unless you're in the same situation). The friend becomes angry or defensive or withdrawn, and you don't understand. If you had checked it out with him before providing a response, you might have discovered that he wanted you to listen, which in itself could help him clarify his thoughts. Or, perhaps he just wanted you to care and respond with compassion. If expectations don't get talked about, both people are disappointed and misunderstood.

Boundaries. Most people would rather understand the boundaries of a relationship than feel like an intruder. In Sandi's case, she answered questions about her divorce even when she believed the question to be none of someone's business. Perhaps she could say, "I'd rather not discuss such a personal question," or "It's too painful to go into, so thanks for understanding," any acknowledgment that she will be responsible for herself. Then she wouldn't be angry with the person for asking or with herself for talking about it. She's free, as is anyone, to talk to people she trusts, and say no to others. No one is obligated to allow himself to be manipulated by people, regardless of their motives.

Integrity. Being related means taking risks and giving a part of oneself. It also means having integrity with feelings, both yours and others'. Sometimes, that means being able to tell a friend, "I'd like to have some space for a while." Distance doesn't have to mean rejection. Integrity also implies that you give appreciation and encouragement to your friend. That's one of the greatest gifts of friendship.

Patience. Giving a person the freedom to grow in his own way and in his own time; being present to another's thoughts and feelings, and even to his confusion, without indifference, is a statement of respect for a friend and his growth. Giving another person room to grow can come only if you can have patience with yourself.

Trust. Caring enough to let go. To trust a friend is to give up trying to dominate or mold or protect him from the lessons of life. Rather than fostering dependency, you encourage letting go, interdependence, and the ability to be responsible for oneself. It's not always comfortable, because you won't know the end from the beginning. It's a daily, step-by-step journey. The other side of the coin is that you can't trust another until you learn to trust yourself, make decisions, and accept responsibility for the outcome.

Listening, feedback, and self-disclosure. These are individual but similar characteristics. It's hearing the truth of another, responding, and telling part of your truth. Sometimes it's confrontation if you feel taken advantage of; it could be a sharing of pleasures; perhaps it's communicating ideas, thoughts, and feelings. The central ingredient is *mutuality*. If it's one-sided, examine the meaning of the relationship. If you're in the role of listening all the time and your friend is the constant talker, you don't have a balance in the relationship.

Appreciation of differentness. Occasionally, you may fall into the trap of believing people must think, react, feel, and be interested in everything you are if you are to be friends. How confining! Even in some churches, people are eliminated as potential friends if they don't agree on a theological point or on how the minister closes the service! You will miss a growing experience if you haven't learned to relate to *different types* of people. This doesn't mean that everyone you meet will become a friend, but neither does it mean that friends have to have everything in common.

Understand that there are different types of friendships. You may have acquaintances you know casually, or perhaps they're potential friends. Some friendships may be limited to meeting certain interests or needs. Golf buddies, carpool and other convenience relationships fall into this category. Friendships that span several years may be based on the mutual history you have between you. These relationships have either grown into significant ones, or they continue out of tradition rather than emotional involvement.

Hopefully, you also have intimate relationships that are based on mutual love and respect for each other. Maintaining a close, growing friendship requires a great deal of energy. If you have a friend who can accept you as you are, he is a special gift. And if you can be free to be yourself, you are giving a gift back to the friend. Intimacy means letting someone see you real. And you can't be real unless you first face yourself. Getting to know the inside part of yourself takes time and work. True friendship is so rare, that if you have three or four intimate relationships in a lifetime, you've had more than most people. Learning to be a friend is an undeveloped art in this rat-race society.

Relationships don't always continue, and saying good-bye well is important. Friends during one time of life may have nothing in common in later years. This may result in conflict, misunderstanding, or emotional distance. Rather than permitting a slow death, talk about the relationship and how you experience it. Perhaps it can be renegotiated; if not, you can deal with the sadness that saying good-bye arouses. Sandi, for example, will undoubtedly say good-bye to friends, who for various reasons, can't handle the change in her life-style. Other friendships die just because people are in two different stages in their growth. Endings and beginnings are a natural fact of life.

Some relationships are or become destructive. That is, you feel worse about yourself, more lonely, and have lower self-esteem in the presence of a certain person. If that's the situation, examining the relationship's effect is imperative to discovering what's keeping you in such a relationship.

Friends are chosen to reinforce the image you have of yourself. As you confront yourself and continue to grow, your relationships reflect that. In most instances, it will mean beginning new relationships, saying good-bye to others, and working to maintain friendships that are intimate ones. During periods of intense growth, you'll discover that you need distance from intense relating. Pain saps energy. If this can be talked about, potential growth and understanding in the relationship is heightened.

Being intimately related means trusting enough to risk, and learning what your friend mirrors about yourself. You will not know everything about your friend any more than you understand all about yourself. Even in friendship, each person is responsible for himself and to God, not to the expectations of others. Choosing to risk yourself can be a journey of discovery. But there will be paradoxes. Where there is intimacy, there is also distance; where there is self-understanding, there is the capacity to offer it to another; and where there is love, there is commitment to another person's growth.

Living Your Loneliness

During the day or week, respond to these questions from your own experience.

1. List the significant friends in your life. What qualities appeal to you in each case?

2. List the relationships that are acquaintances, potential friends, convenient relationships, historical friendships, and intimate ones. Do you wish to work harder on any of these?

3. Are you carrying any destructive or "dead" relationships? Name them. How do you plan to deal with them?

4. What do your friends mirror about yourself? List the traits you see.

5. What is scary, if anything, about *your* relating intimately to someone?

8

Living Your Loneliness

Loneliness can overwhelm you whether you're in the company of others or not. Consequently, some people often run in terror and panic from their fears of loneliness. In order to make the lonely times opportunities for growth, you first must discover what frightens you. You may not be able to eradicate loneliness, but you can overcome your fears, and make the experience one of value.

Loneliness is a fact of life, but it's not a commentary on your self-worth or uniqueness as a person. Try facing in your own mind what loneliness means to you and what's scary about it. You may be uncomfortable with your feelings, but comfort isn't a prerequisite for exploring your fears. If you've consistently used diversions to avoid getting to know yourself, you'll find that developing your own inner resources is the first step in overcoming fear.

One woman volunteered her favorite escape: "When I'm on the verge of panic, I flip on the TV. I've watched it into the early hours when it 'told' me 'good-night'. Occasionally, I'd try to sleep through loneliness, but I'd wake up at 4:30 with a full-blown anxiety attack. That's when there's no escape."

Everyone has escapes. Some people overeat; others watch TV soap operas, become workoholics, enter nonstop activities, go on money-spending sprees, have people constantly around them, try to dull the pain with alcohol or drugs. The possible ways to escape are endless. However, the net result is self-pity and a loss of self-respect. Not being able to live with oneself hurts self-esteem, while learning to face fears is a step toward positive self-regard.

"I first started using my lonely times when I understood what caused them," recalled one man. "Instead of wondering what was wrong with me or trying to run from myself, I used my energy to get something of worth from the experience. I sorted through new ideas, prayed, read a book I'd wanted to read, made key decisions, or reevaluated my goals. It became a time of growth, even though some moments were painful."

The Reasons for Loneliness

Loneliness can be activated by numerous experiences—missing someone special, feeling far away from God, wanting to talk to a special friend. Sometimes, inconsequential events prompt loneliness pain. A sad movie, a poem, or a beautiful sunrise over the lake can trigger a response deep within. Even weekends, when a hectic workweek is over, are times when the lack of a fixed time structure can accent unsettled feelings. It's amazing how much moods are affected by simple weather changes. Rainy or overcast days, snowy blizzards, or the blackness of night can close in on you. Any event which marks the passage of time, such as holidays, anniversaries, birthdays of deceased loved ones, or retirement, may trigger lonely, empty feelings. A monumental crisis is not required to create lonely moments. In fact, the events which are taken for granted are themselves a web of lonely threads: moving to a new city, saying good-bye to a friend, sitting in an airport, bus station, or hospital waiting room. Emotional experiences can flow into lonely reflection. But physical changes such as illness or fatigue also arouse the sinking feelings associated with lonely times. The reasons for loneliness are as diverse as the moods of people.

As one woman stated, "The most devastating loneliness of my life occurred when a college friend and I were reunited after six years. We discovered that the close relationship in which we'd shared all our deepest thoughts had changed. We were in different places—our goals, our interests, our way of thinking—everything was different. She was bored hearing about my job; I was bored listening to her tell about her children's doctor appointments, colds, and new words. What we had in common were past memories. Now, we're unable to bridge the gap between our two worlds."

Understanding the source and cause of your loneliness is the first step in dealing with it. If you discover your unique patterns of loneliness, you can often alleviate the distress. Ask yourself questions. When did the sinking feeling begin? What were you doing? Whom were you with? What were you thinking about? How long did it last? What did you do with the feelings? Your answers to these questions may give you some control over lonely times. However, there will always be some spaces of loneliness. And it's during those times that you can create an opportunity for personal growth.

For example, once you've accepted loneliness as natural, you can direct into positive channels the energy once used to fight it.

One woman kept a journal of her changing moods over a six-month period. By doing so, she discovered not only what prompted some of her lonely times, but also that she handled situations more constructively as she understood ways she wanted to change.

Another man learned that most of his relationships were superficial. When he really longed to talk with someone about subjects other than business, he realized the void in his life. He hadn't developed friendships where he could share the deeper part of himself. As part of the solution, he eliminated some of his extracurricular schedule and spent time with himself. Slowly, as he became more comfortable with himself, he began looking for friends with whom he could establish deeper relationships.

Three women who shared their fears of loneliness with each other set up a plan for living through it. When one of them needed someone to listen or give feedback, she'd call a friend on the telephone. Hearing the caring voice of another human being can be supportive. If time and weather permitted, these three friends met at the park in their warm-up suits and jogged. Physical exercise helped clear out the cobwebs of the mind as well as the joints. Often, a fresh perspective was gained in the process.

All too often, loneliness can result if you live for other people and neglect to achieve a balance with what you do for yourself. Self-esteem is enhanced when you feel important enough to care for yourself well. Go shopping, but not to buy clothes for other family members! Read a book, walk in the park, or go to a museum. Develop your unique interests and act on them.

This isn't to imply that you eliminate being responsive to other people. Not only will you do something for someone else, but you will have a sense of involvement as well. Even listening to a friend (most are stronger on advice than hearing) is a rare gift. The point is to achieve a healthy balance.

Goals Mean Growth

While capturing the meaning and opportunity of today is important, making plans for the future is also necessary. Without a structure, you're at the mercy of your mood shifts. Create short-term (one week) goals, mid-length (several weeks), and long-term (six months or more) goals to provide something to travel toward.

Although poets and painters are well aware of solitude's

benefits, most people are still learning about them. Loneliness can be a source of spiritual, mental, and emotional growth if you accept it and use it to your advantage.

It can facilitate your maturing into a whole person rather than being a composite of roles. Solitude can be used as a time of prayer and of learning to *hear* God and His meaning for your life. He's unpredictable. You never know when you will run into Him through the kindness of a friend, in a book, in a meaningful worship service, or in the midst of your own solitude. You may hear His will by discovering more of who you are and what potential is within you. Prayer is a relationship, a give-and-take partnership. However, many Christians tell Him what they want Him to know, and never *listen* back. They act as though He were the audience for their audition. Perhaps you need to learn to listen lest your tongue keep you deaf! The Lord advised us to "Be still and know that I am God" (Ps. 46:10).

Everyone tends to try to control what's going on around him. In grief situations and times of loneliness, you may shift into high gear with your control mechanisms. Whether you admit it or not, you may want to advise God on what is best for your life. "If I were You" or "It would be better if . . . " are not statements solely reserved for the decisions of other people.

I recall one instance in which a woman experienced the sudden death of her husband. During the lonely isolation of the next four weeks, she received several letters from friends who thought they knew better than she how to live with grief:

"If it were me, I'd stay sedated until the shock wore off. Then I'd face life gradually, as I could handle it."

"Don't let anyone sedate you. The sooner you face reality, the better."

"Take it from one who has been there. Get back to work as quickly as possible. Staying busy keeps your mind off your sorrow."

"If I were you, I'd take a vacation and get some rest. But don't spend the time with relatives; they'll only accent the pain."

"Take some time off and visit relatives. They'll understand and be able to support you through this."

"Whatever you do, sell your house. Memories will kill you. You need a new start in a new environment."

"I hope you can remain in your home. You and Jack shared so much of your lives there."

Is it any wonder that such conflicting advice can be paralyzing? Isn't the same true as you try to advise God on what's best for you? Giving too much mouth and not enough ear and heart is all too easy. To grow and mature in faith requires that you face problems and open yourself to God's involvement. By doing so, you are more prepared to move through hardships and be open to the reality that you will never be absolutely right or absolutely in control. Listen for directions instead of trying to give them. Then you can slowly drop your pretenses, reveal your secrets, and face your lonely burdens.

Learning to ask and hear your loving Father in times of pain is a challenge. It means learning to accept His presence in your life even when you don't feel it. It requires having the faith to know He's there even when life is cluttered. It means having faith even when you're too bogged down to feel a mountaintop experience.

Wherever you are now, you have room to grow and mature. Solitude can be a time when you open up to God those areas in which you haven't allowed Him to move. Each person is a house with many rooms. Some rooms are turned over to God; others you still choose to control yourself. Perhaps in the lonely times you can ask, What rooms are labeled "Private"? "Keep out"? How do you learn to tell Him that which He already knows? How do you let Him into those secret places?

Living Your Loneliness

Attempt to use your lonely moments creatively by discovering your questions for living. During periods of loneliness this week, pursue your response to these questions (write down your answers on a separate sheet of paper as a way to monitor your growth):

1. What are your usual escapes from loneliness?

2. Name several of your patterns for loneliness. Do they occur in the evening, early in the morning?

3. For each one, write down how you will provide a structure for yourself or how you will use the time.

4. During what times do you most like yourself?

5. In what areas do you want to grow in your prayer life?

6. What are hidden areas that you protect from God? Become more comfortable with acknowledging them to yourself.

7. Identify several goals for the future:
   a. Short-term (one week)
   b. Mid-length (several weeks)
   c. Long-term (six months or more)

9

God's "I Love You"

A butterfly is the final product of a life of growth and struggle. Every butterfly that flutters on a spring day is a statement that in order to live you must grow. But growth, even for the butterfly, doesn't occur overnight. It's a process. The stages begin with the egg, then the caterpillar, to the pupa, and then to the graceful butterfly. At each point, it had to give up the security of one stage before going on to the next stage. Because of fear of the unknown, some people choose to stay at the caterpillar stage. They don't realize that the loneliness of refusing to mature can itself be a frightening experience.

One of the most beloved passages in the Bible is Psalm 23. The whole range of man's experience, from birth to death, is reflected in these verses. It is a statement of God's promise to be present through all circumstances of life.

Times of crisis and trouble always breed loneliness. When the bottom drops out from under you, you discover whether or not your faith really makes a difference. The answer to that question depends on what kinds of expectations you take with you through the valley experiences of life. If your expectations are visions of what ought to happen, you may experience intense disappointment. In fact, you may be blinded to what *is occurring* by concentrating on what ought to happen but isn't.

Religion doesn't make everything easy; it doesn't necessarily make problems smaller. One of the people at Baylor University who greatly influences the lives of students is the Associate Dean of Students, Virginia Crump. She is one of those rare people who can hear people where they are and, without condemnation, encourage them to be more of what they can be. Hours of her day are spent helping students, when by the time clock her workday is over. Her ability to accept people is a gift, probably even more so because she is seldom without physical pain herself. For at least 10 years and 12 operations, she's lived with arthritis. She's endured tears, questions, depression, anger, and sometimes gratitude. During the dark moments of her agony, she's searched the Bible, ministers, friends, herself, and God. She's learned in her own valley experience that sometimes problems must be lived with. All you can do is "keep on keeping on."

She's still reaching students and living with pain. But her question has changed from "Why?" to "Why not?" The last time I talked with her, she was preparing to speak to a student organization. Her topic? "God in My Life." No, she doesn't have all the answers and, in fact, probably still has many questions. But she lets God be God and is open to Him. The only way out is through.

Saying yes to God may mean strength to continue. Prayer is openness to what God gives as He deems appropriate. Virginia Crump doesn't hide from life waiting for tidy answers. Nor has she become embittered because of unmet expectations that she had for God. Instead, she continues to live life as she finds it in the context of looking upward.

A group of nurse trainees were asked by their supervisor at the beginning of their hospital induction, "How would you want to die if you had a choice?" Most of the responses were similar to "quickly" or "painlessly" or "in my sleep." The supervisor made no comment, but at the conclusion of their training in the ward for terminally ill patients, she again asked the question. This time the responses were different. The students had learned lessons about life by working with dying patients. Instead of being afraid of death and its pain, the nurses had experienced another side of the coin. Their patients had been given time to take care of unfinished business, see friends, and work through their impending death with their families. The nurses who first had wanted to die suddenly had discovered benefits in having time to prepare.

Learn to Say, "I Love You"

You may be tempted to call on God only in times of trouble or when your own resources fail. God is then an answer for your lack of preparation in faith. You may explain circumstances away with "it was God's will" when, in fact, you may be using that as a way of *not* growing in faith. How often have you used God's will as a way *not* to be involved in someone's pain, or not to deal with questions that haunt you? One man, whose wife had recently died, was asked by a friend how he was doing. Before he could respond and voice his feelings of loss, the friend said, "It was God's will. Accept it." This friend then walked away as if to announce that he didn't want to be involved. Granted, the man will eventually have to accept that his wife is dead, but perhaps he wasn't able to yet. Instead, he may have needed a friend's arm on his shoulder, and words or caring support.

Some need to learn how to say, "I love you." Have you ever stopped to think how many people never hear those words? You may assume it's said in families, but many family circles are emotional deserts when it comes to verbalizing love. Or, you may think that expressing affection will be viewed as improper or overly involved or unmanly or too risky. "I love you" can convey a hopefulness about life. Christ was God's "I love you" to the world, the ultimate message of hope. I remember one woman who, during a small group experience, said, "I can't remember the last time I was told that I was loved. It might have been when I was a child." This woman was facing an uncertain future. Love is a powerful antidote for loneliness and fear, if only people will learn to express and accept it.

These Are the Good Old Days

Traveling the valley experience requires courage to face feelings of hopelessness. Quite frankly, most people are usually more comfortable talking about the weather or the energy crisis than talking or hearing about personal difficulties. Yet, not only is presence important to a friend living with loneliness, but it's a necessity for *you* as you struggle in your own periodic valleys. It's ironic that you may fear love's claim on you, yet desire it so keenly. You must learn to shed your pseudosophistication and speak love as well as try to act it.

Christ accepted persons as He found them, and encouraged them to look honestly at their lives (John 9:41). Sometimes faith calls you to be involved in the struggles and the pain of others. God's gift of faith and grace is interwoven in the experiences of your life. Whether you are facing your own pain or responding to the hurt of another, God provides you with strength for the circumstances. His grace isn't given in advance to be hoarded. Rather, it's a gift given as it's needed. Remember, "I shall not want."

Psalm 23 is a process of life marked with growth and character development. It doesn't encourage living in the past or the future as a way to escape present realities, however difficult.

Robert, a fellow Christian, provides an example of someone who was married to the events of his past. He grew up in a family that offered affirmation for achievement. While he was grateful for the appreciation he felt, Robert also experienced a sense of frustration. Sometimes, his father wanted too much too fast in areas that were more important to him than to Robert. Robert stayed on the treadmill through college, medical school, and during his residency. As he began the process of deciding where to locate, and whether to become associated with a hospital or go into private practice, Robert became increasingly depressed. At a time of life when all his hard work was paying off, he felt let down. There could be many explanations for this. But what Robert discovered in time was that he went to medical school to please his parents. He'd had only passive interest in the field, even though he had the aptitude for it. Now he faced the alternatives of putting his training to use in a career that he chose but was not his choice, or disappointing his father by deciding not to practice medicine. How enormous is the influence of the past on the present! Robert had been living the inner novel of his life, and now didn't like the plot. He can face his own feelings of disappointment and learn what has controlled him. Or, he can live a life of anger and resentment. Robert's past, if he deals with it, can become a friend, regardless of his future career decision. But how lonely the experience is, claiming himself for Christ, in spite of family demands in the past.

Living in the past is not the only way to try to escape present circumstances. Some try to live as if the grass is always greener somewhere else. They face life by anticipating tomorrow. Neither the past nor the future can protect from today. The writer of Psalm 23 encourages maturity through both the good and the tragic events you face.

What are your expectations for the valley experiences of life? Do you expect God to bail you out of threatening circumstances, or are you open to receive His grace in whatever form He gives it? Sometimes Christ protects us, not from the realities themselves, but from what our fear of them can do.

It's the cynicism, despair, hopelessness, and temptation to quit altogether that results from fear.

Alienation from God or disappointment in His grace is one of the most painful forms of loneliness. It drives you to redefine your identity and discover what you really value. You may examine your goals, your hopes, and your memories. As you relive scenes in your past, you'll remember words of love, jabs of criticism, even missed opportunities. If you settle for just weathering these moments, you'll miss an opportunity to gain new insight. But if you settle into your loneliness, you'll discover an invitation to wrestle with spiritual growth.

Living Your Loneliness

During the day or week, respond to these questions from your own experience.

1. What butterfly stage are you in?

2. When do you call on God? What are typical times for you?

3. Can you tell those people what you love about your feelings? Why or why not?

4. During the valley experiences of life what are your expectations of God? Of yourself?

10

Life as a Gift

Loneliness can be a significant experience in which you evaluate your limitations and discover your gifts. Most people live with an underdeveloped appreciation of their potential and an exaggerated estimate of their weaknesses. How they view themselves shapes how they view life in general.

Life is a gift, but many have hardly opened the package. They ask what to do with it, or where to put it, or of what use it is, or what the gift will be like five years down the road. It's as if they expect the will of God to descend from the sky on a giant cue card! Yet, the gift itself is an opportunity and, by opening it and peeling back the layers, you can discover your directions. You will learn how to discover the gifts that are unique to you.

Learning about yourself is expensive. It means submitting to the loneliness of introspection instead of copping out to an escape. One of Jesus' most piercing questions was, "What will a man gain by winning the whole world, at the cost of his true self?" (Matt. 16:26, NEB) Within each person is a self to be developed and fulfilled.

The first step is to be open to yourself and your awarenesses. To be human, with constantly changing roles, is not easy. Frequently, people move from mask to mask, replacing one only after they grow tired of it. Jesus frequently parted from the crowds to ponder, sift through His thoughts, and listen to the wisdom of faith. The times of solitude were when Jesus faced Himself.

As you spend time with your own thoughts, you'll embrace an inward journey that will include an examination of several important principles. It is wise to remember that everyone starts at a different place in their growth regardless of how similar their surroundings and families. Consequently, to compare yourself to another person demeans your uniqueness. What occurred in one family may have a totally different implication in another one. What is easy for you to achieve may be more difficult for someone else. But that doesn't mean the other person is inadequate. It means only that you have different gifts and are at different places. Celebrate the value of diversity, for all are learners from each other.

A Bridge to Reality

At first glance, the limits question appears to be negative. However, in actuality, it's the bridge to reality and living creatively.

Elizabeth, a woman in her 40s, recalled an encounter with her limitations. "All my life, I have planned to go back to school, get a degree, and make a contribution with my life. I daydreamed about being a great author, teacher, doctor, or even an engineer! But I was always too busy doing other things. On my 40th birthday, it dawned on me that even if I accomplished any of those feats, it wouldn't be in my youth as I'd planned. I also realized that my potential doesn't lie in those areas at all. I faint at the sight of blood; math is difficult for me; I don't want to teach 35 kids and then face my own four at home; and my spelling is atrocious. It occurred to me that because I've spent half my life dreaming about things I really don't *want* to do, I've not discovered and developed the things I *can* do. So, I decided to face the fact that I will never be another Adela Rogers St. John or Saul Bellow or Ernest Hemingway, and to put my energies into being more of who I am. It's taking time, but at least I'm no longer hiding from myself."

Everyone has limitations whether they're physical, mental, educational, or emotional. Facing them frees you to grow in areas where your potential is dormant. You can turn a deaf ear to yourself or you can listen and grow into more of what you are capable of becoming. Either way, you are responsible for your decisions and the resulting consequences. Even indecision is a decision. If you allow decisions to be made by default, eventually this will paralyze your ability to take risks.

A man named John learned early about responsibility, or his lack of it. When he overspent his budget, he blamed the IRS for robbing him. When his marriage entered a crisis stage, he blamed his parents for urging him to marry and settle down. When his children misbehaved in school, he blamed the teachers and counselors for being incompetent. Eventually, he had problems on his job, so he was critical of his co-workers. His boss called him in to discuss the issue, and John listed the faults of others without mentioning his own contributions. After hearing him out, his boss fired him. Not, he said, because the problems on the job were all John's, but because he wouldn't tolerate someone who so easily blamed others and wouldn't accept responsibility *for* himself. When the shock and sadness of the loss wore off, John began to see himself real and understand his role. The price for the insight was heavy and painful, but it was a beginning.

As he examined how he related, John realized that when he got into a situation he resented, he reacted much as he had as a child when his parents disciplined him. He hadn't updated his style of relating, so he fell back into childhood blaming whenever he experienced threatening circumstances. If we can learn from our past and deal with it, we can better *choose* our directions in the present.

Growth is motivated by pain, and fulfillment is dependent on our ability to be self-affirming. To be aware of your limits increases your capacity to live with your unique realities. It puts you in touch with your finiteness. However, coming to terms with your humanness also involves appreciating and using your gifts.

Frequently, however, people are more in touch with the darker side of themselves. Think about it. Most are more aware of what they don't like than what they *appreciate* in themselves. You need to learn to put an arm around your shoulders and pat yourself on the back. Claim what you're proud of and what you've done well. It's vital that you learn to be a friend to yourself. You don't have to do things perfectly in order to take credit for them. Acknowledge what you feel good about.

This will require that you learn to listen to your feelings. You may have grown up not learning to take feelings seriously. You knew things churned around inside of you, but you weren't encouraged to express what you felt. Now you must learn that how you feel gives you a message about yourself, and about the quality of your decisions. Your mind has the capacity to rationalize, but your stomach won't! In times of decision-making, listen to your gut reactions as well as to your logic. They give signals as to what's going on around you. In fact, God can speak to you on the inside as well as in external events.

Learning to appreciate your gifts means that you will be called upon to develop them. And using them will involve learning to be self-affirming as well as learning to fail successfully. Society has placed such a premium on success that many run from fear of failure. Although failing is not comfortable, it teaches lessons in the process. Sometimes it means you are not on the right road. Or, it may signal the need for reevaluation. The loneliness of failure calls you to reexamine yourself, but it's not a statement about your worth as a person.

One woman was so afraid to make mistakes that she seldom took risks. Anything less than perfect to her meant that she wasn't a good Christian. To underscore a point, I told her that I made at least four major mistakes a week and was working up to five. She looked stunned, and then said, "You mean you actually think it's OK to make mistakes?" There's a difference between a license to do anything without a moral structure and the opposite pole of living in fear of failure. Living on either extreme stunts your growth.

The meaning of life is not in success or failure but in how you choose to respond to the events. You can become harsh and cynical, or you can guide the painful parts of life to growth. Lessons about success and failure and the use of your gifts can be found in the parable of the talents (Matt. 25:14-30). Many feel that they have no talent if they can't readily identify it. If you don't sing or write or head corporations, you may feel there's nothing to discover. Often, you may be given gifts for different times in your life. Yet, understanding and accepting your gifts can be a lifelong struggle. You are busy searching for something different, even though no one knows what it is. You miss your gifts of the present because you are so busy being dissatisfied with what you do have. Scripture doesn't comment on how the man with one talent views the world; that's no excuse for mismanagement! It merely indicates that he's responsible for his life and what he does with it.

The meaning of gifts begins in self-acceptance. Learning to be yourself is a truism that sounds good but is difficult to practice. You have learned that being real means taking risks. So you may settle for being phony and the loneliness that results.

Acceptance encompasses feelings, thoughts, actions, ideas,

even questions. It's learning to try to see yourself just as you are and then valuing yourself.

Where many people get caught is in comparing themselves to other people. You see people you went to school with become presidents of corporations. Or you read with interest about names making the news in research, politics, literature, or whatever. Perhaps you learn how a poor fellow became a financial wizard, all because he bought thousands of acres when they were only pennies an acre. During times of other people's success you may say, "I'm not making anything of my life. I'm not making an impression on the world." And your mind churns with questions. Are you doing what you're supposed to be doing? Will it make you famous or rich? So what? What will be the rule for *your* life?

You can't fake self-acceptance. You either practice it by the minute or you put yourself down by comparisons with other people. You'll miss the opportunities present today if you don't accept yourself as you are.

Certainly, it can be a lonely experience if you've never faced yourself. To risk knowing yourself requires a special kind of courage. You may not even know where to begin if it's a totally new experience.

Look back over your life. Has anyone ever accepted you unconditionally? No bargains; no if onlys; no ifs, ands, or buts. You didn't hear, "I'll accept you if you'll do this," or "I'll like you if you'll stop doing that," or "You're OK if you don't cut your hair or shave your beard." Being acceptable as you are, warts and all, is a memory that will help you face yourself. You at least have a track record to get you started.

One of the messages Christ gave was in the power of acceptance. Because He knows the good and the bad, the light as well as the dark sides of each one, He calls you to a clearer sense of who you are. In doing so, you can begin to ask yourself, "Is this person, job, or vocation really good for me?" You may find that you and certain individuals are mutual enemies. You have added a dimension of acceptance that calls you to realistically examine your limitations and potential.

You can't be given a gift unless you're willing to accept it. The antidote to an inferiority complex is learning to accept yourself. That in itself is a gift, both to yourself and to other people.

In the confusion of life, you have the need to be heard. Yet you may not have learned to listen to others or to yourself. Prayer is a beginning—learning to *hear* God and His meaning. Through the process of using lonely times for growth, you discover your gifts and move toward wholeness. Other people's expectations and your own fears lose their ability to mold you. Certainly, how people respond affects you, but you don't have to live in fear of rejection. Nor do you have to spin your wheels counting your talents and comparing them with those of other people. In fact, the only appropriate comparison is in relation to how much of your potential you are using. After all, life is a gift but sometimes you have to look for ways to receive it. Learning to live with loneliness five minutes at a time is one way to accept yourself for who you are.

Living Your Loneliness

During the day or week, respond to these questions from your own experience.

1. Identify traits that describe yourself.

2. What are your major disappointments or shattered dreams?

3. Describe your limits as you see them.

4. What parts of yourself have you not accepted as being OK?

5. Identify some things you've done well or that you take pride in.

6. What do you dislike about failure? What can you learn from failure?

7. Who gives you your definition of success? What is it?

8. Identify your talents or gifts. What do you do with them?

11

Acquainted with Grief

One of my early memories as a child is of the events surrounding my great-uncle's death. Relatives had gathered for the traditional Christmas party, and the usual merriment was in the air. Shortly after my family had left the party and gone home for the night, we received a phone call. My great-uncle had suffered a massive heart attack while at his daughter's house. He died before he could be rushed to a hospital.

He was from a small country town, and that was where the funeral was to be held. I remember climbing the steps of the front porch and walking into the house where so many memories lived. As my parents, sister, and I walked in the day before the funeral, I was stunned to see the body of my uncle in a casket. I turned and asked, "What's Uncle Brad doing in the living room, Mother?" She explained that was the custom in smaller towns that didn't have funeral parlors.

As I looked around, I saw my cousins and other close relatives surrounding my great-uncle's wife. Everyone seemed to do whatever was natural for them. Some were crying; others were talking; a few were silent. The reality of the sudden death was beginning to sink in. During the course of the next few hours, many memories were recounted. Stories were told about my uncle, questions that were raised by children were answered, and people expressed their loss.

Obviously, times and customs have changed, both in positive and negative directions. But one of the lessons I learned from that whole experience was that death and grief are a natural process of life.

It contrasts quite differently with another experience involving a woman with a terminal illness. To survive, she lived in a hospital room and was connected to tubes, needles, and machines. Doctors and nurses referred to her as a terminal patient, rather than as the mother of three, a wife, and a daughter. During the days before her death, she expressed her fears. "It's not dying or what's on the other side that's frightening. What scares me is being alone, and not knowing *how* the end will come."

The hospital has replaced the home as the place for dying; the medical staff has replaced the family in being there for the final good-byes. One of the prices we pay for advanced medical technology's ability to prolong life is that the death experience has become even more lonely.

Certainly, the medical staff does provide important health care, and they need ample room to provide emergency treatment. And in the case of prolonged illness, it's not always practical for people to die at home surrounded by their family. Frequently, work responsibilities, geographic considerations, or medical factors such as controlling the pain make it imperative that a person receive treatment in a hospital. In such cases, families often contend with unnecessary guilt; God understands the circumstances involved.

Dr. Elisabeth Kubler-Ross, an authority on death and dying, has encouraged changes in the American style of dying. Dying at home, when possible, is one of her suggestions. Greater education for the public and the medical staff is another, for death is not failure. Perhaps learning to die well, whenever that time comes, is an important goal. You can face dying a little at a time by learning how to let others grieve. One of the most helpful ways to help families deal with loss is to permit them to be part of the process.

As one husband said at the time of his wife's death, "We were all there: her parents, our daughters, all of us. When she breathed for the last time, her face looked peaceful. It was the first time I'd seen any relaxation from pain in a year. We knew that we'd miss her, but finally she was with God."

All of us have felt the loneliness of wanting to support someone in a crisis but not knowing how. In the case of sudden death, help can be given to the survivors. Usually, terminally ill patients inherently know they are dying whether they've been told or not. Different clues give this away, as well as an unexplainable feeling the patient has. Nervousness and increasingly brief visits by the doctor or family or friends is one clue to the patient. Nervousness or an overcautious selection of topics to talk about are other clues. One woman said she knew she was dying when people started trying to do for her things that she was still physically capable of doing for herself.

Serious illness raises a number of questions for the patient. The person begins to replay memories and wonders if he's made a contribution with his life. Often the age of a person indicates whether he feels that death is an intruder on goals, or whether life has been a long journey. However, age can be misleading. A friend, in trying to console a dying man, said, "But at least you've had a full life. You're now 65 years old!" The man angrily responded that he'd lived long but not well. He hadn't accomplished all he'd wanted to in relationships, in his vocation, or with his children. One of the things he did on a day out of the hospital was to spend time with his children, and to say some of the things he'd always wanted to but hadn't.

Other thoughts plague the person. He will no longer be

with those he cares about. Even Christians with the promise of heaven must deal with the feelings of loneliness and loss that death brings.

Fears become questions. "Will I be a burden?" "How much pain will there be?" "What will the tubes and machines do to my body?" "Will I die with dignity?" Some of this can be dealt with by doctors telling the patient of his condition, if there are no psychological contraindications. The patient and family have a right to know the truth, and to ask any questions that concern them. Every question may not have an answer, but an honest "I don't know" is better than the patient feeling he can't ask.

Stages of Death

If the dying person doesn't want to talk, don't press. Be sensitive to what he says as well as what he doesn't want to say. And remember that since grief is a process, you may see a person during several stages. According to Dr. Kubler-Ross, the first stage in dying is denial. It's a healthy reaction, allowing the person and his family time to take in the message. This coping pattern may begin with a person saying, "I can't believe it," or, "I won't believe it." You come face to face with the fact that illness or death isn't something that happens only to *other* people. This same reaction is common with people who undergo surgery, have amputations, or lose the sight of an eye. It's an intensely lonely period, when a person develops his defenses to move through reality.

When the shock wears off, anger or resentment may surface. "Why?" accompanied with blame or even guilt ("What did I do to deserve this?") are evident. God or the doctors or nurses may be blamed. God can handle the reaction; you can be helpful by hearing the person without judgment. Rushing in with answers will only serve to block his process into the next stage.

The third stage is bargaining, a temporary truce to find a way out. The premise is that promises will be fulfilled if only more time is given. "If You'll give me another two years" becomes a time of saying, "Yes, I realize this is where I am, but . . ."

From bargaining, the person moves into a stage of depression. Now the full reality is present. Acknowledgment brings depression and a preparatory form of grief. Hopefully, the family, *who is also going through some form of this same process,* can be involved with the person. Frequently, the patient is ahead of the rest of the family in dealing with grief.

Eventually, the time comes to face death. The patient who has passed through the other stages can accept the reality. It's not a happy time or sad time, just real. The stage of acceptance may be a difficult time for family and friends. If the patient withdraws, as often happens, they feel cut off or wonder, "Why doesn't he talk with us? What did we do wrong?" You can help the family understand that when the patient has no need to see someone, it indicates any unfinished business with that person is complete. If the family can look at it in these terms rather than look for reasons for rejection, the patient and family can begin to let go.

Suicide

One of the painfully lonely realities is that regardless of how much you care, you can't solve anyone's problems for him. You can grieve *with* a person, but not *for* him. This is most graphic during times of suicide.

A woman in her early 20s shot herself when she visited her parents one weekend. The grieving father, stunned by Ann's death, repeatedly asked, "Why? Why did she do it? She had so many years left. I'd gladly have carried her problems on my shoulders if I'd known."

It's difficult to love someone and be involved, knowing you can do nothing to ease their pain. The father's grief couldn't be eased; words could not erase that Ann chose death over life. What became evident was that this father had to live with his own burden, but he couldn't carry it alone without friends.

Ann's suicide was a powerful, tragic statement about her life. Death was not the greatest threat for her. Instead, the significance and quality of her life posed the biggest obstacle. She must have felt a living death in a life crowded by her own pain. How do you respond to those left behind? Obviously, pat answers serve no use. Perhaps it calls each of us to come to grips with our attitude toward death and life. Suicide is not the answer, but it has increasingly become a choice people have made looking for a way out.

Regardless of *how* a person dies, the issue is the same. Length of life is not the measure of who were are. Life is a process of letting go, for we face inevitable losses during the continuum between birth and death.

A Comforter

If you are trying to offer support after any kind of death experience, the best gift you can give is the ability to listen. Listening may not be in the form of words; it may mean being present to the person and whatever is going on—even silence. Understand that the stages of loss are *normal*. It in no way means a person has less faith just because he asks questions or becomes angry or depressed. Jesus wept at the death of Lazarus (John 11:32-37), and suffered through questions at His own execution. Sometimes, comfort is given by grieving with a person or hearing the questions. If you can provide a person with the atmosphere to be whatever he feels, unconditionally, you've offered the gift of support.

Not everyone can do that because they haven't learned to grieve through their little deaths of everyday life. No one becomes suddenly accepting or compassionate or sensitive. If you want to learn how a person will handle the presence of death, you have only to look at how the person handles his life.

If you're in the role of comforter, help strengthen the reality of death in the minds of the living family members. Some help deny that death has occurred by saying, "He's gone" or "Don't be upset—he's just out of sight." Encouraging such fantasies is not helpful to the grieving person. The family must reorganize their lives without the member who died. If death occurred from a terminal illness, the family may have completed their grief work. That means that the natural feelings of anger ("How could he leave me?") and guilt ("I should have shown my appreciation when he was alive," or, "If only we hadn't had that argument") that occur after a sudden death, may not be as intense. However, the shock, sadness, tears, depression, and reorganization stages of grief still must be worked through.

Being realistic about loss is a beginning. Tears are an honest expression of loss as well as a helpful way to move forward with life. Encouraging stoicism with statements such as, "For the sake of the kids" or "Christians are happy" or "Be strong" prevent acceptance and the necessary expression of loss.

Most people deal with their anxiety of wondering what to say to a family by saying too much. Sensitivity at such a time requires listening and an honest, simple expression from you. "I'm sorry" or "I care" is adequate. Saying that you understand usually is met with resistance. After all, you are *not* in that person's shoes. An arm around him or a pat on the shoulder is a nonverbal cue that you really care and are present.

Don't go to extremes, however. Being present is one thing; hovering over a person so that he has no privacy is quite a different matter. Preaching about the will of God and how He gives strength, or explaining why death happens will not make the griever feel better. It may make *you* feel better. But the sorrowing family needs the comfort of being with people who don't ask probing questions, or carry on nonstop conversations. The Christian *knows* about the strength God grants; the non-Christian will feel the meaning in your words when he can hear them, and he is the only one who knows when that time is.

During death experiences, immediate structure is necessary —food, childcare, small ways of showing love. But six weeks after the funeral is when the loneliness can be devastating and when the shock has totally worn off. It's then that a person may want to ask questions about what went on during the time prior to and after the death when he was in a fog too thick to see clearly. Thoughtfulness and personal availability are important then and on special occasions such as holidays, anniversaries, and one year after the death. Sometimes, a person will choose to spend those times alone, but a card or phone call will say you care and you remember.

Respond to grief and needs as sensitively but as openly as possible. Often, people refrain from talking about the person who has died. Yet one of the gifts you can give is to recall for the survivors memories that are special. Talk about the person who died, tell stories about him, include the funny as well as the touching anecdotes. Express your own feelings, that you miss him or remember him. By *not* talking about it, the griever wonders if you miss the person, and if you can understand his grief.

God, as a loving Father, taught being present to people at their point of pain. He offers understanding and a capacity to hear people where they are. Your ability to be a comforter has much to do with how you have learned to respond to the little griefs in your life, and how you relate to your own fears of death. Hopefully, you can learn that grief is a healthy part of beginning again. Loneliness is a part of the process but doesn't have to be the end result. The lesson comes from Christ: grieve, but not as people without hope.

Living Your Loneliness
During the day or week, respond to these questions from your own experience.

1.What is your earliest memory of a death experience? What did you learn from it?

2. What little griefs in your life have prepared you to act as a comforter?

3. Use your solitude to explore the following questions that are appropriate to your own situation in life.

For the Formerly Married

a. What were your expectations, both realistic and unrealistic, that you had for marriage? Rather than putting your marriage on trial, attempt to understand what went wrong and learn from it.

b. What were your needs at the time of your marriage? What are they now? Needs change with time.

c. Are you living your life through other people—children, friends, parents? What interests can you develop as you assume responsibility for yourself?

d. What expectations do you have for yourself and other people? Are they realistic?

e. What are your goals for life now (what *you* want). What are your values? Where does God fit in?

For the Married

a. What has been your chief disappointment in marriage? Chief benefit? Can you share it with your mate?

b. What are your needs now as opposed to the day of marriage? How do you meet them?

c. What in your relationship makes it tough to be real with each other?

d. List four things you appreciate about your mate. About yourself.

e. Name one goal for your marriage over the next year. Where is God in it?

For the Never-Married

a. What is your chief disappointment, if any, in being single?

b. List the advantages and disadvantages of being single.

c. What are your goals for the future? Are you making marriage so much a goal that you postpone living your todays?

d. Name those who are your extended family. Are you developing meaningful Christian relationships? If not, how can you meet people?

e. How are you giving to other people as well as receiving? Where is God in your life?

For the Widowed

a. What is your current structure for each day? How are you living with lonely times?

b. What have you learned about yourself since the death of your mate?

c. How do you request help from friends or family members when you need it?

d. Name those people who care about you and have offered their support.

e. List one goal for yourself over the next day, or week, or month. How does God enter into your process of setting goals?

12

Living Your Dying

Obviously, you will face times, if you haven't already, when *you* will need the comfort of friends. If you've not experienced the death of a loved one, just wait long enough, you will. Everyone becomes acquainted with grief in time.

In the midst of sorrow, you may often wonder if your feelings and responses are normal. Do other people react like this? What *is* a natural process of grief?

Shock, tears, guilt, anger, depression, an intense sense of loss, wondering if you can make it through the pain. Overwhelming loneliness and a desire to withdraw and be alone. Lack of energy or interest to participate in social events. Wanting to talk to someone yet not thinking anyone can *really* understand. Physical symptoms of the distress and stress you're experiencing. Any or all of these feelings may be a natural part of your grief.

Some people, including Christians, may have questions. How could God allow this? Why would a loving Father permit such pain? Anguishing questions burn in your mind. The Bible is full of this kind of concern, with no attempt to avoid the religious implications. Read the Psalms, or follow the grief process of Job. When he lost his children, his possessions, and his wealth, he cursed the day he was born. Learning how to lose is one of life's most important challenges. Job's loss was so profound that he could find no meaning in life. It was as though part of himself was dead.

He looked for explanations, as did his friends, who decided that Job must have some unconfessed sins to warrant such catastrophe. Yet the calamities of life are mysterious. The more people try to explain them and fix blame, the less they learn.

Eventually, Job faced God and was reminded that what he lost wasn't his in the first place. Everything that was his was a gift, not a possession. Because Job allowed himself to ask questions and feel the anger, resentment, and even the guilt, he was able to confront his beliefs. It was no longer the innocent response of one unacquainted with hardship. He had a trusting relationship with his Father that permitted questions. Job learned that he didn't have a right to things or people or feelings that were gifts from God. The fact that he was blessed these ways was a gift from the Father. But Job had to go through his own process, from darkness to light. That doesn't happen with a snap of the fingers. He couldn't know the end from the beginning. His faith grew into maturity as he struggled with the mysteries of God at work.

The experience of loss can embitter a person forever. Some people hate God, the world, and themselves and resolve never to be vulnerable again. Defiant rage is one alternative. The other option is to permit the feelings and the questions, and learn to look at life as a gift. Those who travel the latter path can gain a deeper perspective of faith and a greater sensitivity and flexibility about life.

Job moved from *acceptance* of the losses to a stage of *actualization*. He raised the question, What do losses mean? Then he re-entered life. He moved back into the world based on the limitations and insights he discovered

How do you handle your grief? One man played the role of a stoic, unemotional tower-of-strength during his father's funeral. Everyone thought of him as brave and supportive. Because he made all of the funeral arrangements, called people to notify them of the death, and cared for his mother, he didn't have time for his own grief. Six months after the funeral, he collapsed. When, by your actions, you encourage the suppression of grief, stoic acceptance becomes a sort of role play. A smiling depression often results when grief work is delayed.

What about Guilt?

You may experience certain natural responses to death's wound. Guilt is characteristically part of grief when death closes the door on unfinished business. "If only . . ." thoughts may plague you for a period of time. One woman lived with guilt over not preparing her son's favorite meal before he returned to college after spring break. He was killed in an automobile accident on the way back to school, and his mother lived with "if only" thoughts for months. Guilt in search of a cause will always find one. And it may not necessarily be related to major acts that hurt the one who died.

Guilt is not a feeling only related to death experiences. One man wounded his son in a freak hunting accident. The rifle was prematurely fired and hit his son in the eye. This father tried to talk about his guilt with friends, but they encouraged him to suppress it with statements like, "Well, at least your son is alive." The father, wracked with pain, talked to his minister. In the course of the conversation, he exploded with "I wish he'd died. Living, he's a walking monument to what I've done." The minister replied, "Yes, you made an enormous mistake. I can understand why you feel so guilty." The father burst into tears, sobbing uncontrollably. Finally, he could let out his emotions. Thanks to a sensitive minister who didn't encourage him to pretend, he had permission to deal with his feelings. That was exactly what he'd needed to continue his grief work, someone whose words wouldn't block his movement through the process. He'd already sought God's forgiveness, but he hadn't been able to accept it because he couldn't forgive himself. And, he couldn't forgive himself until he could deal with the loss.

Another natural response is to make a person bigger in death than they were in life. Idealization only encourages more guilt and loneliness. You can't feel OK about a past relationship with someone who is larger-than-life in your memory.

A third common reaction is to feel an emotional responsibility to the one who died. "What would Mother want me to do?" "How can I complete the work he started?" are not unusual questions. As you move through the grief process, the effort to be bound to the loved one becomes less of a chain.

Exposure to grief forces you to confront the reality of your own death. Sometimes that occurs in developing symptoms like those of the person who died. More often, it just brings your fears into focus. You don't control life; you can't choose to live forever; you can't even select how you'll die. In reality, everyone is terminal. *Terminal* is usually associated with a malignancy or detected disease. But even when you are healthy, you're terminal. You don't have an indefinite hold on life on earth.

To acknowledge that, and accept it, allows you to live freer with the anxiety associated with death. You can learn to deal with the little losses so that you are better prepared to live with the major ones. When you learn to face death, you then can be free to truly live in the present. Most people are so afraid of dying, at an unconscious level as well as consciously, that they program their lives with busyness to avoid dealing with it. It's paradoxical. When you learn to live with death, then you can truly celebrate the time you have. To become more comfortable with your humanity and better acquainted with grief, expose yourself to a variety of experiences: do volunteer work in a hospital, routinely visit a cancer patient, use your lonely times to face your fears, spend time on a farm where birth and death are viewed as natural parts of life, or learn from a friend currently going through a divorce.

In some ways, divorce is more difficult than a death experience because the corpse is still walking around, and society doesn't know how to be helpful! Many view death as having a nobility about it. Not so with divorce. The grief process in a divorce is the same as with death or any other significant loss, regardless of how the decision to divorce was made. By being part of other people's experiences and dealing with your own times of loss, you can learn to face your own death a little at a time.

Questions about death are shrouded with mystery. But the Bible clearly says that death is a new beginning. Christ has already paid the price. The meaning in the mystery is that heaven awaits you beyond the grave.

One woman, a Christian with the courage to face herself said, "I know I'm dying, and I'm in too much pain to *feel* the joy of my faith. But I know it's there. I've seen the seasons change for 44 years. They'll continue their march after I'm gone. That's how certain I am of heaven and the hope that awaits me there." The night before she died, she was propped up in her bed singing hymns and folk songs. The last time her family saw her, she was singing, "Sunshine on My Shoulder," followed by "Zippity Doo Da"!

Faith is the courage to live your dying, face the questions, and accept the tension between meaning and mystery.

Living Your Loneliness
During the day or week, respond to these questions from your own experience.

1. Think of your most recent experience with personal grief. What questions did you ask God?

2. How do you feel when you get angry?

3. How do you handle your grief?

4. If you currently feel guilt, what's the cause? How do you plan to deal with it?

5. Have you made anyone bigger in death than in life? If so, what steps are you taking to "see him human"?

6. What scares you about death?

7. Have you planned for your own death, i.e., prepared a will, talked to your children about realities of death, etc.? Why or why not? When do you plan to?

8. How do you feel when you think of yourself as terminal? Why?

9. List ways you plan to become more acquainted and comfortable with grief.

10. How do you respond to people experiencing the grief of divorce or the death of a loved one? What is the Christian response?

13

Life Is Problem-Solving

In this success-oriented society, you may get caught up in other people's expectations for your life. You rush on a treadmill, trying to keep up or get ahead. In the process, crisis, loneliness, and trouble are viewed as obstacles to goals you have set. A successful life is unrealistically defined as one free of trouble, and made the ideal.

One way or another, you learn that life is problem-solving, and not a mythical happy-ever-after time. You discover that developmental crises are a part of living; that you may be in charge of your children, but you don't control them. Loneliness in some form comes to every man and every woman. You're responsible for your choices, but that doesn't mean you have total control over the events in your life.

It appears that you must learn to travel two roads if you are to live as though today is the "first day of the rest of your life": the road of gratitude and the road of forgiveness.

A woman of great sensitivity once shared her fear. "I have no reason to keep going. I've accomplished the goals I've set for myself, but I feel empty." She'd spent years thinking that accomplishment would give her meaning. Instead, she discovered that achievement doesn't fill the void of loneliness. And brooding over the way things are only feeds feelings of alienation. When she began to see life as problem-solving, she laid aside her fantasy that if you just accomplish enough, you won't face difficulty or hardship.

The stance of gratitude is the ability to accept life as gift, not as obligation. Resources are always available in the midst of a crisis if you try to find the five loaves and two fishes in the situation. When Jesus asked His disciples to feed the crowds, He used what He had available rather than bemoaning life as He found it.

In your lonely times, think of the five loaves and two fishes in your life. For what can you express gratitude? Often the things that are the most special are the most taken for granted. For example, you have a memory, which means you don't face tomorrow in a vacuum. You have the choice of forming relationships if you can risk vulnerability. And, how about the necessities of life, good books, the ocean or mountains or growing grain?

The difficulty is to find or feel gratitude in the midst of crisis or loss. During illness, career changes, or when dreams are shattered, friends move away, or a family member dies, you have to learn to be grateful. It's being grateful when you don't feel like it that will show you the five loaves and two fishes present (Matt. 14:17-19).

Jesus understands the loneliness of struggling alone to face painful uncertainties. Many times you can't change circumstances. You can only involve yourself in the situation, let it teach you its lessons, and grow to accept the situation as a challenge. Gratitude in the midst of crisis or uncertainty is not easy.

Perhaps you don't know how to say "thank you." You are more adept at expressing appreciation for the beauty of life than you are for unpleasant realities. Perhaps you want things *your* own way or not at all. To know that you don't have to be infallible to be loved is comforting. You don't have to be without stains and sins and mistakes to be acceptable to God.

A man fired from his job was given a curt explanation, "The rising cost of inflation." As he focused on the immediacy of the problem, he said, "There's no way I can thank God for this experience. How can I care for my wife and two daughers? I don't see how *anything* good can come from this experience."

Six months later the man had another job and reflected on the last six months of his life. "I haven't enjoyed the fears and insecurity I've felt. But, I think our family has learned some important lessons. In some of my most bleak, lonely moments, my junior-high-age daughters were able to reach out to me in a way unlike any other time of our lives. Because I grieved openly in front of them, they didn't feel responsible for our problems. When one of them asked if things would be better if they weren't such a burden, I clarified that immediately. We talked *with* each other instead of *at* each other. We reaffirmed love and family ties. And they were reassured that my grief was not because of anything they did or didn't do. Children can deal with a great deal when they're allowed to participate in the grief process instead of being 'protected' from it! When I look at the whole six months instead of only the events surrounding my job loss, I can appreciate some things in the total experience."

Gratitude begins when you can see life as a process rather than as scattered events. When you focus on one situation, you only have tunnel vision.

The flip side of gratitude is forgiveness. By whatever name you call it—imperfection, sin, failure, mistakes, regret—how do you handle it? Some people internalize failure and make it the measure of their true being. Eventually, it leads to self-contempt and lonely self-doubt.

Another way to deal with evil is to blame other people. Rather than dissatisfaction being internalized, it's externalized.

Other people are scapegoated as being responsible for whatever is wrong. The classic example is of the scribes and Pharisees who would have stoned the adulterous woman, if it hadn't been for Jesus' intervention (John 8:3-4). Everyone, at some point, has given other people "credit" for his own large or small mistakes!

Jesus provided another way to deal with sin. He understood forgiveness as an event, not merely as an idea or concept. He relates in a stance of acceptance and unconditional love. Forgiveness is available, not because of what you are, but because of what God is. You have the choice of making life a prison of self-doubt and anxiety or of living it fully on the road of forgiveness.

Now that sounds all well and good. But, you may be one of those who, even in your lonely times, think forgiveness has to do with other people. You don't view yourself as all *that* selfish, for you have done the best you can "under the circumstances." You don't see yourself as particularly insensitive. After all, it's your turn to have someone be sensitive to you! So you have catalogued your sins or you live so much in the past or future that you miss the opportunities of today. Hopefully, if the shoe fits, you can learn to seek forgiveness in between crises as well as during them.

The roads of gratitude and of forgiveness are essential for the Christian. Each one comes into and leaves this world alone. In between, you face the loneliness that is part of being alive. Lonely times can be spaces of solitude and increased sensitivity. But the gift of life can be best understood and accepted if you can learn to be thankful when you don't feel like it, and to ask for forgiveness even if you have forgotten how or why you should.

Giving assent to loneliness, accepting it, and growing from the experience is itself a process. The gift of life is an act of love. And when there is love, there is also loneliness. How are you living with yours?

Living Your Loneliness

During the day or week, respond to these questions from your own experience.

1. What are the five loaves and two fishes in your situation?

2. List those things for which you're grateful but take for granted.

3. Can you say "thank you" for one thing during a present unpleasant reality in your life? What would it be? What's stopping you?

4. Finish this sentence: "I only feel acceptable to God when . . ."

5. List three people you want to affirm for being in your life. How do you plan to let each know of your appreciation? (Mail, phone call, visit?)

6. Name something you don't forgive yourself for. How long do you plan to carry the baggage?

7. You've been given the gift of life. What are you doing with it? What are your goals *now*, as you begin another day of living your gift?